Pen to Paper

Pen to Paper

*A NOVELIST'S
NOTEBOOK*

by Pamela Frankau

Doubleday & Company, Inc.
Garden City, New York
1962

Dedication

*TO M. K. WHOSE NOTION
IT WAS; WITH MY LOVE.*

Contents

Prologue

ANY NOVEL

ONE

THE IDEA

It comes without warning. I have been watching for it; sometimes digging for it, searching back among old files in my memory: the only files I keep. Here are to be found a number of books I have wanted to write and have not yet written. I say 'to be found'. Not always; not all of them. The files are haphazardly maintained. It is only when the rhythmic creative restlessness comes back that I turn them over, to see what I've got there. My thriller with the pretty title . . . The novel that runs through one day only . . . The light comedy about the Wonderful Old Lady who was really a stinker . . . ?

The odds are that the creative mood will have none of them. Its hunger is there but it preserves, for all the hunger, a dictatorial appetite. It has taken about a year to grow. The end of the last novel left me, as usual, mentally bankrupt, empty of purpose; seriously doubting I could do that again. In youth it was different. The new idea was forever intruding before I'd finished with the old one. Those were the days, I say to myself now, the good old days. (Not the good old novels. Still, I thought they were—in that lost age when the beguiling Next hurried me on.)

The tanks take longer and longer to refill. I wait stoically. Because of the doubt in my mind, I am not entirely happy, no matter how good life may be. I am ill-at-ease with any work that isn't my chosen trade.

I can be busy. Indeed I must be busy. First, because I can't be idle unless I'm in France. Secondly, because I have to earn some money. So the interim period bustles by, and if I could ever believe it was only an interim period, that would be all right. A year of reading for the Book Society; a string of broadcasts and lectures; occasional articles and short stories: all fairly good fun in recollection and most of the work worth doing, but almost on a level with cooking, which is something I enjoy and can do reasonably well.

Nine or ten months of the interim period deepen my mood of mistrust. I cannot believe that I shall write another book. I remind myself that I have written thirty. And although, at fifty-two, I have far more to say than when I was young, I seem to have far less to say it *about*. At this gloomy stage, I am certain there's no new subject for a novel and that, even if there was, I wouldn't find it.

Then, mysteriously, I am past that stage. I am awake and prowling. The tanks have refilled. The listener who lives inside has ready ears. And presently catches a sound upon the air.

This experience is difficult to record. All I know is that something stirs, comes alive and appoints a rendezvous. Even the 'something' is hard to identify. It has, in its time, been many things: a fragment of talk overheard; a place; a person; a phrase with no known context; an old memory; a line of poetry. Once it was the look of a small graveyard in Bristol.

The vibration is unmistakable, though at its first coming it can hardly be called an idea. It is merely a clue: a flutter-winged clue. (And best not to hunt it down too eagerly. Taking an occasional glance over my shoulder, I wait for it to come nearer, to move in.)

The magic can die out at any time. What looked like the breath of life on Thursday may turn to dull dust by Friday afternoon. This can come of staring, plotting, figuring, pressing too hard. But, most disconcertingly, it can come for no reason at all. The lights that went up so suddenly can go down as fast; and that's that.

Only twice in my life has the whole concept of a novel come immediately, imperatively, the lightning striking all in one day. As a rule it walks warily, taking its time, becoming slowly visible by way of the clue.

When the idea to which the clue has pointed takes shape, the shape is always human. One person, two people, three perhaps, with their ragged beginnings of life and their blurred destiny. They collect company, background, behaviour as they move in.

Nothing to do now but hold them 'with a hand as light as a butterfly'; resisting the temptation to make notes, the temptation to force on them any preconceived or practical clothing. I must keep my silence and stick around. They will gradually give me a clearer glimpse, a wider perspective, and presently they will come up with what looks like their story. Incomplete, full of gaps and question-marks, but still story enough for me to take a conscious hand in it. Growing bolder, I harry and probe at the matter before me.

Notes made at this moment have one outstanding characteristic. They look quite meaningless: a series of jottings in gibberish. Given time, they expand; they take the appearance of long letters written to myself. Some of the letters are interrupted by practical reminders from the world outside, such as 'Hey, what about the laundry?' (Disconcertingly different from Henry James' *'Come to me again, O mon bon'*.) Feathering back through the private communications, I have found that my most frequent instruction to myself before I sign off is 'Brood, now . . .'

This is testing-time. If I can walk away from the desk and go about my factual life still with the sense of holding a nugget in my hand, still accompanied by the new invaders of my solitude, all is well. But I am still in danger of writing a new idea out of existence with too many notes, even of 'brooding' it out of existence. Once there was a deliberate synopsis made before I ever let myself begin. Now there is no synopsis at all. A rough story-line, beginning, middle and end, with a few scenes that have become sharply visible on their own account: this is the most I dare provide for the characters. A session of really detailed planning and the whole lot commit suicide, taking the novel with them. It is with the lightest of equipment that I set out on my first draft, the Rough.

The precarious ride from the first clue to the beginning of the Rough may last many weeks. On the way I have to renew my vows of silence. In the rising excitement, with the dream unrolling in my head, it is too easy to talk. And talking is fatal.

Burbling, using the person closest to me as a sounding-board, on the two-way understanding that the board makes very few sounds, is helpful; (better than talking to myself, a thing I now do regularly, pacing my study floor.) But this is for one person only. (Not more than one, after all, would be likely to suffer it.) To the temptation of the sympathetic, intelligent customer asking 'What's it to be about?' I dare not yield. The longest reply permissible is one sentence. (As with my last novel I could answer 'A boy who lost his memory' and endanger nothing.) This is an old rule. I broke it in the year 1939.

The occasion was a small, civilised party and the current novel was safe, I thought, in my head. The synopsis, the habit of those days, was complete. The characters were alive and kicking: the story was all there. The theme was superstition and I had done much entertaining research-work with spiritualists and fortune-tellers. Tomorrow I would begin to write the Rough. I had just confided this consoling fact to a woman who said instantly 'Do tell me all about it.'

I hesitated, only for fear of being that bore, the lover who talks of the beloved. Did she, I asked, really mean what she said? Was she sure? She said she did and she was.

In our quiet corner, I went ahead, not at great length, but with a sketch of the characters and their situation, tak-ing them on through the beginning, middle and end (as I can do now, any time after the Rough is finished.)

Except that I didn't get to the end. As I told this story I found that with every word I spoke, it lost its truth, it lost its ring of magic; it lost all, all. A crude, melodramatic tale, every character cardboard, every situation contrived . . . what the devil, I said to myself, did I ever see in this? I looked at my listener. Wasn't her interest well on the wane? I thought so. She still looked sympathetic, but in a different way, as though I were describing to her an illness or an accident which had overtaken me.

I began to run down. Hopelessly I heard myself saying 'Well—*then*, in the middle of a tremendous thunderstorm, the brother arrives . . .' and I stopped. She waited politely. But horror and misery had quenched me altogether. I looked her in the eyes. After a moment I said 'It sounds perfectly awful, doesn't it?'

'Do you want me to be honest with you?'

'Please.'

'Sure?'

'Sure.'

'Well, then—yes; it does sound perfectly awful.'

I didn't begin it next day. I didn't begin it at all. My talking had killed it stone dead. Had I kept silence, I might have discovered in due course that this book wasn't worth writing; or perhaps that it was; I shall never know.

TWO

THE ROUGH

I acquired the two-draft habit after twelve years of tidying up as I went along. In one extreme period of affectation I would polish every page so neurotically that no single correction was allowed to appear. If a correction came up, I would begin the whole page again. The result was the prettiest manuscript I ever turned out and although I soon ceased to admire the novel I was sad when, by a family misunderstanding, the four hundred beautiful pages went towards the war-effort as waste paper.

What I slowly discovered was that the impetus of the story slackened with the tidying-up process. It seemed more intelligent to go full speed ahead while still on fire: then back, in more temperate mood, for the rewrite. At first I was plagued by all the mess. The scribble, the gaps, the balloon-attachments, the spatter of X and ? in the margin haunted me. But since that beginning, the two-draft habit has become routine. There is, I think, only one disadvantage: a fountain-pen.

('Where's your typewriter?' asked Mr Butler, bringing the clean clothes on their wire hangers and a certain amount of snow into the living-room. The 1950 winter on

Martha's Vineyard brought few interruptions to work: Mr Butler was one of them. I was glad to see him. Looking up drowsily from the table with the scattered foolscap and the overcrowded ashtrays, I said 'Typewriter? I don't have one.' He began to look sad for me as if he thought I couldn't afford a typewriter. I added, 'I mean, I don't use one. I can't type. I never have.'

Mr Butler seemed a little dazed. ''Mean—you write all that out by *hand?*'

'Yes; twice.'

'Twice?'

'Well, the Rough and the Smooth, you see.' It hadn't struck me until this moment that for every book a hundred thousand words long, my hand must write two hundred thousand. I was thinking rather smugly about the physical achievement when Mr Butler said in a reproving tone: 'Henry Beetle Hough, the editor of the *Vineyard Gazette,* —he has two typewriters,' and went out into the snow-storm.)

Besides neuralgia, rheumatism, arthritis and fibrositis, I have a permanent callus on the middle finger of my right hand. When I get to the end of the Smooth the callus is swollen and hurts. So do my eyes, my head, my neck, my back and my arm. My writing becomes less legible every year, which is tough on the typist who, incidentally, becomes more expensive every year. I could save myself much ache and much money by learning to type.

But I am set in my ways. The way of the Rough is this:

On the day after the danger-signal has gone up, telling me that if I brood and make notes any longer this novel will die stillborn, I sit down with a new foolscap book in front of me and go into what must look like *rigor mortis.* I am putting on my diver's helmet. I am about to go down and find out. I take a long time. If titles came to me easily I should, I think, write the title out for fun and and turn another page. But I am a martyr to title-trouble and I can rarely name this child in embryo.

I adjust the straps of the helmet. I look at my notes again: merely a nervous gesture, I need nothing from them now. Least of all do I need the jolting glimpses of problems unsolved, huge question-marks, 'THIS WON'T DO' interrupting a recorded train of thought in angry capitals. I put the notes away.

There is, as every writer knows, all the difference in the world between the dream itself and the committing of the dream to paper. For weeks I have been strolling around comfortably with these people who are in my head. My knowledge of them has grown. My affection for them is strong. Yet I haven't, I know, really met them. The meeting is just ahead: *now*. Here we go. Blowing a last kiss in my mind to the magic of the dream-stage (it will never come back, it is infallibly and irrevocably ending right here) I plunge.

A tentative Roman 'i' and the first sentence scrawling below: *At nine o'clock Alex Wharton came to the house* . . . I know, roughly, the shape of the scene: I know what I want to happen in it. But the hazard is made by Alex Wharton, by Geoffrey Bliss and the rest of the cast. The whole purpose of the Rough is to meet the people on paper. The easy-going shapes who have come to a certain measure of life in the dream, will now take on three dimensions; acquire flesh and blood and minds of their own.

The story-line, is, as I have said, of the thinnest. And here I am no longer a diver, but a mountaineer. This line might be a rope that I have thrown around the rocky profile ahead. I have made fast the belay on the other side (which is more than a mountaineer could do before he began the climb.) I have a working notion of the way the climb must go, for me to get there. And that is all.

Should somebody penetrate the barbed-wire entanglements of my handwriting and read my Rough, it would make little sense to him. He would find bewildering changes of time and place. The people would confound him with sudden new characteristics. Some would change their looks. Some would be whisked away without explanation. Some would put in a late appearance, yet be greeted by the rest as though they had been there from the beginning. He would find, this reader, traces of style followed by no style at all; pedestrian phrases, clichés, straight flat-footed reporting. Here a whole sequence of scenes complete and next some mingy, skeleton stuff with a burst of apparently contemptuous hieroglyphs on the blank left-hand page beside it. Nor is the left-hand page reserved for 'Exp' (meaning Expand), 'X' (meaning Wrong), '//' (meaning much the same as 'X' only more so) and '?' (meaning what it says). The left-hand page is likely to be a shambles, taking afterthought insertions for the right-hand page; paragraphs whose position may not be indicated at all. No; a reader would have no more fun with the Rough than the writer is having.

My advice to myself in all the weeks and months of the Rough is to keep going, keep plodding along. There are intermittent rewards on the way: when the right words come, when the characters begin to put on weight. At the desk I must strive; in my mind I must not. No snag suddenly struck (how, for example, did he get there the day before he started?) must turn into a worry. Make an 'X' and get on.

What I need next is something I can neither force nor

foresee: the moment when the novel clicks, with the sensation of gears at last engaging. At this moment I know that, although three quarters of the work still lie ahead, there is a book here. It's alive on paper; it has got its own move on. The moment is unpredictable. I may write more than a hundred pages before it happens. (For anyone who reads my books, I will add that I remember the precise moment where it happened in my novel *Ask Me No More*. On page 89, when I began to describe the opening night of the five-star flop written by the playwright Geoffrey Bliss. Up till then the book and I had just been staggering hopefully along.)

I have written a Rough in three months; I have likewise taken nearly a year on it. The working-hours vary: anywhere between four and ten hours a day. Two absolute rules abide.

Discipline is the first. Self-discipline,—not, I think, my strongest point—yet representing the only hope at this stage. I must fight certain devils, outside and inside. The devils outside will always beckon and sometimes win: bright sunshine, cricket, the *Times* crossword, a luncheon date . . . But the devils inside are the worst. Sheer listless reluctance; pain; worry; the flat morning mood; a sudden lust for new clothes; deep melancholy; wild happiness; bad news; good news; all contrive to threaten the second life that I must live from day to day.

The number of people who have said to me since I was nineteen, 'I imagine one can only write when one feels like it' merely sets me wondering if I have *ever* felt like it. Discipline alone makes the hand with the pen move; keeps it moving; sees to it that the snail-pace of the morning accelerates by afternoon.

The other absolute rule is protection. Every Rough I've

written has needed protection and not only from the devils. It is a subtle affair. Not a matter of regular hours, nor even of sitting still in the same place. I have protected the Rough while flying the Atlantic, while driving across France and meeting many beautiful interruptions by the way.

What, then is the procedure? Mainly, I think, evasive action. Certain company should be avoided. The company of the devitaliser, that friend who takes from life rather than enhancing it, the mental blood-sucker, the strong marauding personality. The early-morning chatterer on the telephone. The disorganised chaos-bringer. The one who wants a long, serious talk. To be avoided also,— the swaddle of the Sunday newspapers, the opinions of agitated atheists, the gin-and-tonic before lunch, the reading of novels or book-reviews. The correct literary diet alternates the Gospels with Whodunits.

Conversely, there are stimulants to be taken. The theatre is almost always a stimulant and a movie (in the evening) the best stimulant of all, I don't know why. Evening parties do no harm; the drink towards the end of the day, unlike the fatal gin-and-tonic, has a definite value. This I have discovered in the last ten years. The discovery still interests me.

By six o'clock the engine is running down. Because I am tired, I am fumbling and bumbling and getting nowhere. Soon I call a halt and read back. No good. I begin to fuss and tinker, despite stern instructions to myself to stop it. (All right, so you put 'X' in the margin opposite the second paragraph on page 209. Nothing new about that, is there? The faulty paragraph directly influences the scene you are writing now? Well, it would . . . Nothing new about that, either. Oh, *don't* go back, for heaven's sake . . . get on.)

Let me illustrate this private dilemma. My 'X' indicates

that A. did *not* come in from the beach, still wearing his swimming-trunks, as I have written. He couldn't, because, on second thoughts, this must now be a day of pelting rain. But I have let the paragraph stand. Beside the 'X' I have noted that I must substitute 'Walk or drive or something'. But here, twelve pages on, A. is having his showdown talk with B. He is telling B. (he must) what happened on the beach. But, hell, it *didn't* happen on the beach and by now a chunky section of crossings-out indicates my inability to sail into the 'walk-or-drive-or-something' background as though I'd already established it. (A hurdle that I can take in my stride when I am not tired.)

Six-thirty. Time for a drink. Pushing back my chair I go in search of the ice. In my head I am still fussing. I pour a scotch-and-soda, and carry it back to the desk. Before the drink is finished, I have found a solution to that plaguing 'X'. Something else is happening, too. The drink is setting a number of prisoners free; I wasn't, until now, aware of their captivity. Up from their tightly-locked cells down below, there come ideas as well as words, a valuable store that has accumulated, I believe, all day.

This is not merely a matter of having acquired the drink-habit at evening. It is no illusory drunkenness, no mis-guided exhilaration. The discoveries I make on the first drink are always right; inevitably, they hold good. They will survive with scarcely a word altered, in the final draft that is still so far away.

But I must beware of taking a second drink if I want to go on writing. I am usually saved by the necessity to cook the dinner.

The older I get, the more positive I become that the end of the Rough is the best moment of all. My eternal doubts, my abiding lack of confidence will not be hushed until then. Even after the 'click' I cannot be sure that I can finish this novel. I never have been sure; I never will be. I am, I feel, slowly pushing a knot towards the end of a bit of string. I cannot know that this knot will finally unravel. I have long ago lost my mountaineering metaphor. The plunging diver is forgotten. There is just the knot in the string.

Yet now, at last, it is happening. I am making more speed with these chaotic, indecipherable pages; some of them, indeed, grow quite legible as the pace quickens. Next week, perhaps . . . In the notebooks the daily letters have shortened. A laconic '16.30 hrs. That's that and now for the scene on the tower' may be followed by '18.30. Done it.' There are also some private, smirking observations wherein I pat my own back. (All notebooks, by the way, are rigorously destroyed when I come to the end of the Smooth.)

Well, one day or another day, here we are. Galloping home . . . *home*. Solemnly I print THE END, a childish habit whose pleasure I cannot deny myself.

I am entirely, marvellously happy.

What I have on the desk is a pile of foolscap books, running to about four hundred largely illegible pages. These, and my notes. Weeks, months of rewrite are ahead of me. There are hideous problems still unsolved. But in my head all is well. The story runs; the characters are uproariously alive; enduring company. We have come halfway together. They have shown me what they can do, and what they can't or won't do. Best of all, I needn't part with them yet. I still have my two lives.

And confidence has come. For the first time, I am the boss around here. The novel is safe, safe, safe.

Like many moments of purely selfish happiness, this one should be kept to myself and my Thousandth Man. But I rarely keep it to myself, because I can't. Not even after the warning in Westchester County, some years ago.

I had just printed THE END. But I had no time to indulge the happy stupor, because I was due to dine elsewhere. Despite my sense of dancing on a rainbow, I doubtless galumphed into the room like a slap-happy carthorse. 'You must forgive my not having changed,' I said to my hostess. 'I didn't have time. And I'm not really fit human company because I'm too excited. I just this instant finished the rough draft of a novel.'

'Well, now isn't that thrilling?' said the nice lady. 'And is it published yet?'

Never mind. I have reached the age when I know quite certainly that listening is a lost art. (A curmudgeonly view, particularly from anyone who talks as much as I do.) And in the glow that surrounds the end of the Rough, all can be forgiven.

Now is the time to look it through, to set up the notes in synopsis, chapter by chapter, for the rewrite. And to tackle a few of the arrears outside: letters, income-tax returns, medical attention, clothes. I try to take a two-week breather before I set out on the Smooth. This is the longest that my impatience will allow.

THREE
THE SMOOTH

Things have changed. Among them my state of mind, my approach to work and my time-table. Four hours a day could content me while I worked on the Rough. Now the minimum is six; more often I write for eight or ten hours. Because of my handwriting and the pending typist, I must go at it as neatly as possible. This slows the pace. But the longer day and the complete confidence give the Smooth a predictable lifetime: five months at most. As I work, I realise that the Rough was more fun than I thought; there wasn't the obligation to keep my eyes on—as it might be—two saucepans and the oven at the same time.

Usually I digest and memorise the immediate notes before I begin. They are severely practical, impersonal notes now. They will include the results of factual research. (The most demanding of these, in my recollection, were the processes of sculpture that I had to learn for a novel called *The Winged Horse*,—barely outlined in the Rough because then I was still learning.) The notes will also point to the insertion of new scenes: each requiring a Rough of its own before the rewrite.

But, by and large, magic has taken over. The discoveries

go on. Again I find that some random, seemingly-pointless part of the Rough has acquired authentic value. It relates to the book in a way that I could not have foreseen. It can comment on a situation I hadn't thought of; it can give me the sweet surprise of thinking 'I builded better than I knew'. It can also provide surprises of a comical kind.

('What the hell are *you* doing there?'

I had spoken aloud. The room was a room in Palo Alto, California, and the novel was called *The Willow Cabin*.

I was two-thirds of the way through the Smooth. Turning up the first page of Book Three, Rough, I saw that somebody called Brett Arnold was strolling down Hollywood Boulevard. He was a complete stranger to me. It was like coming into the dining-room and finding a burglar at the sideboard.

'*What—?*' I said again in an outraged voice; then I remembered. This poor Brett Arnold, who made a few tentative appearances in the Rough, had long since suffered a sea-change: emerging as quite a different person named Jay Brookfield. It was hard to believe that Jay hadn't even existed in the Rough. He was now an important character, at home in the first two books of the Smooth, fully equipped to work out his further destiny.

Well, time for Brett Arnold to be going, and Hollywood too; the background had moved up the Highway to San Francisco. Though I had no compunction in liquidating Brett, I was sorry to lose the Hollywood scene. This, I saw, had some good stuff in it. 'Save that' I told myself. ''Come in useful another time.' But this I knew was an idle instruction. I have never been able to save anything; neither money, energy, nor the 'good ideas' that some writers are careful to store in notebooks. Foolish, but like most bad habits acquired over the years, a permanent disability.

27

I wouldn't know what happened to that Hollywood chapter.)

However long the working day with the Smooth, I am unlikely now to find that the evening drink reveals hidden resources. Sometimes it can help, in polishing an awkward phrase; sometimes it can bring an elusive word to mind. But this stage is congenitally in need of a cool head and strict, watchful eyes. Last chance for clarity, last chance for euphony, last chance for surgical skill and architectural repairs.

My head, my eyes, my arm and the rest are now in trouble. I hurt all the time, pretty well everywhere. But the temptation is to go on too long and so lose valuable perspective. Discipline begins to prove itself quite differently . . . in knowing when to stop.

Protection too has taken a different form. I am immune to the alien influences. All I have to protect is the time spent at my desk. No more Atlantic flights, no journeys in France. The Rough illustrates perfectly the fact that writing is a portable profession. I can carry on with it anywhere. I have written it in dentists' waiting-rooms, in casinos, in trains and at the hairdresser's; in a B.B.C. control-room with 'Woman's Hour' coming through from the studio, biding my time for the operating-theatre, sitting in a bar, watching by a deathbed.

But the Smooth demands a long solid surface of desk or table, with a rigid attendance upon the notebooks, the Rough and the clean foolscap before me. Here all goes softly, even the hard rows still to hoe. The cast of characters play at the top of their form; as their director, my task simplifies.

Presently I begin to look ahead, to see the end of the journey appointed by that vibration, that knowledge of a

rendezvous, many months ago. I can at last hear myself
admit that I am finishing a book; instead of mumbling 'Oh
—sort of . . .' when asked if I am working just now. The
world outside begins to take on a future importance.
('France . . . in May? That would be nice.')

I am ruthless with my physical self; with my aching and
my disturbed, diminished sleep. Whole days are spent in
the tobacco-clouded room, never putting my nose outside
the front door for a breath of true air. My company and I
have better things to do. And although I am so soon to part
with them (perhaps because I am) we have never been
closer in union. They are mine and I am theirs. My second
life is at its peak. It has sucked the reality out of my factual
existence. Vividly haunted, I come straying into pale rooms
and meet pale acquaintances. ('Well, as a matter of fact,
I'm on the last lap of a new novel.')

So it comes: the day that was invisible, the moment that
I never thought to live. Nothing can stop this being the
day when I shall print THE END again, more carefully this
time. And then,—'*That's it!*' as the T.V. announcer snaps
at the winning point of the tennis match. I shall take the
last book of the Rough and hurl it across the room. And
afterwards . . . but there have been interruptions, even on
this day:

'Oughtn't you to be getting ready?'

The words had to be spoken twice before I took them in.
The place was the South of France in the spring of 1951
and the book was called *The Offshore Light*. My least popular novel and my favourite child, it had fought me
'mounted and standing' for years. Borne on the air in 1940,
it had hung around. Other novels had been written while,
faintly and disturbingly, it remained in view. Now, from
nearly a thousand pages of Rough, I had at last distilled

29

the Smooth: not more than three hundred pages in all. And I was racing towards THE END; three pages to go. I should be a little late for lunch. Oh, what a beautiful morning . . .

'I said—oughtn't you to be getting ready?'

Dragged back, I blinked upon my friend. I became aware of other sounds beside her voice. I was writing, as I had written for weeks, at a table in the bar-lounge of the Hotel St Christophe, Miramar-par-Théoule. The French radio was tinkling. Down in the alcove, beyond the glass doors, Madame at her desk was giving instructions to the head waiter. Upstage left, the kitten was attacking the cat.

'Getting *ready?*' I repeated bemusedly, 'I'm . . .' Here words failed me and I made sawing gestures with both arms above the matter on the table.

'We are lunching with Dash and Blank,' said my torturer.

'*Since when?*'

She reminded me. Dash and Blank lived in a beautiful house built on the rock-point, five minutes away from our hotel. I cut her short:

'You go' I said, 'Say I'm sorry but—'

'You can't do that. It's a party . . . You can't—'

—'I can' I said, with some expletives let in. By now somebody had turned up the radio; probably one of the two Frenchmen carrying inscrutable brief-cases and ordering Cinzano. The kitten-cat controversy had become a clinch, with screams of pain from both parties. A gust of wind slammed the glass doors, left ajar.

'Dear God' I said; and other things.

'You can finish as soon as we get back. What's the difference?'

One more burst of Anglo-Saxon and I surrendered. Hugging my load of paper, in a temper unusual to me, I went to my room. I changed my clothes. Sullen beneath the blue sky, the green pines and the gold mimosa, I tramped beside my companion; in whom by this time my mood had provoked a fit of giggles. It was all quite intolerable. I was sure she had invented the luncheon-party. We should find Dash and Blank alone, informally-dressed, undemanding. Food wouldn't be served for hours and I would sit drinking on the terrace; just my body sitting there; all the rest of me left behind on the Island of Leron, in the book, where my second life was.

'Damn it,—I could have been *late*, couldn't I?'

'You are,' said my friend. 'We were asked for one o'clock and it's half-past.'

True enough. Six more guests were well ahead of us on the terrace. Pulling myself together, apologising politely, I tried to behave. And, halfway through luncheon, received my reward.

'How much longer will you be working on your novel out here?' asked the civilised gentleman sitting opposite.

'Never a bit of luck like this again,' I reflected as I answered thoughtfully, 'Oh . . . about twelve minutes.'

The end of the Smooth still stuns me. It is the moment of triumph, with an enormous sadness running concurrently: desolation because they are all gone. ('The whole book suddenly toboggans away out of sight' as Lettice Cooper puts it.) I found this, written two days after the moment of triumph, while I was destroying the notebooks:—

'For months and months THE END has been the peak of an impossible mountain, the place I'd never get to. Finishing a book was the thing that happened to other writers. Here I am, then, where I longed to be. I'd forgotten (I always do forget) that the air would feel so empty, that

31

there would be nobody here. I look around my head and see that every one of them has tiptoed quietly out.

'How can they be so dead and so gone? Lying flat and still, in eight red foolscap books and one black box . . . They're no longer the people who have kept me crowding company for months and months. They are the characters in a finished novel. I have no more concern with them, nor they with me. And I miss them abominably.'

But this is the necessary way to feel, the way I must feel. This is proof of work completed. Should the people stick around, keep their places in my mind, the book's in trouble. I have missed something, overlooked something; there is still work to be done.

How, Why and Where

CHAPTER
ONE

'I should warn the reader' says Somerset Maugham in his last book of essays, 'that the author, treating of an art he pursues, is biased. He very naturally thinks his own practice best. He writes as he can, and as he must because he is a certain sort of man; he has his own parts and his own temperament, so that he sees things in a manner peculiar to himself, and gives his vision the form that is forced upon him by his nature. He requires a singular vigour of mind to sympathise with work that is antagonistic to his instinctive prepossessions. One should be on one's guard when one reads a novelist's criticisms of other people's novels. He is apt to find that excellent which he is aiming at himself and likely to see little merit in qualities that he himself lacks . . . This unreasonableness would be unfortunate if writers were few, or if the influence of one were so great as to compel the rest to conformity; but there are thousands of us. Each one of us has his little communication to make, a restricted one, and from all these communications, readers can choose, according to their inclination, what suits them.

'I have said this' he observes at the opening of his next

paragraph, 'to clear the ground. I like best the sort of story that I can write myself.'

It is some years since I planned, a little against my will, the lectures for a creative-writing course to be given at an American university. Fate saw to it that I never gave the course. But I have a record of the stipulations I made for it, and part of the opening paragraph seems to me to link with Maugham's thoughts on the subject. I wrote:—

'I cannot teach anyone to write. Because nobody can be taught. A writer is (to coin a phrase) born and not made. And a writer like myself is made up of many convictions, which, should he meet them in somebody else, he would call prejudices. In the years of practising his trade, he has made for himself certain rules. He has come to certain conclusions. Inevitably, he holds strong views on the technique that he has evolved. His own tricks are the ones that he finds best for his purpose.'

I went on from there to explain that my rules for writing fiction could be rejected wholesale by any other novelist. I could, I said, offer no more than a course in the writing of fiction as done by me. I should be using myself as a guinea-pig throughout.

It is so, now: I am this creature for the purpose of this book.

What do I, as a reader, ask of a contemporary novel? Somerset Maugham has given you the answer. I ask for the fulfilment of my own aims as a writer.

First, I must be involved, engaged, made to believe the makebelieve. The jargon that has given us the term 'reader-identification' wouldn't, even if it expressed itself in English, mean what I mean. It is only while writing that I need to identify myself with characters; not while reading. But I must believe that they exist. I, the reader, must be an absorbed spectator, a privileged listener, that old 'fly on the wall': seeing and hearing all that passes: temporarily persuaded that these things are in fact happening to these people.

The surest way to preserve this illusion is for the novel to develop itself in immediate, visual scenes. I want to be shown, not told. Should a chapter begin:—'The next five years were fruitful ones for Lindsay' or: 'As the weeks went by, Roy found himself surrendering more and more to the charm of Oxford,' then I am being told, not shown. The writer has intruded, like a master of ceremonies, to make an announcement.

He can even disturb my illusion a little by writing: 'Dinner was a silent, uncomfortable affair,' or: 'It was typical of Jones to walk to the station instead of taking the bus.' He is commenting again; I can hear his voice. If he wants to tell me about the uncomfortable dinner, I would rather see it happening, or hear one of the characters allude to it. *Was* it typical of Jones . . . ? Then what I need is enough perception of Jones for me to make the 'typical' comment in my own head; or, alternatively, to hear one of Jones' fellow-characters saying 'There he goes, saving threepence on the bus-fare as usual.'

My second demand is a story. This doesn't mean a complex plethora of plot, nor any frequent, explosive action. By a story I mean a situation that moves onward, drawing me along with it; a condition that unfolds and reveals. The whole book could concern itself with the moods of a man immobilised in a hospital-bed and still do this: still give me a beginning, a middle and an end.

My next request concerns itself again with the illusion. Though I feel no need to identify myself with the characters in the story, I want to be with them, watching them, listening to them at close range. There is one way by which a writer can make it hard for me to sustain the belief. That is by asking me to identify myself with more than one of them at a time. It happens when he jumps around in presenting the thoughts of his characters, moving too rapidly from head to head. This way:—

'As Joan waited for Robert, she was acutely conscious of her shabby suit, her battered shoes, her whole look that must tell him at once how things were with her. When he opened the door she saw the same prosperous, assured Robert; the big, blue-eyed man wearing his fat smile and his good clothes.

'Robert stared at her. He couldn't believe what he saw and he didn't want to believe it. Poor old Joan . . .'

The illusion has gone. I am at once aware of unreality. Why? Because the writer has switched me too quickly from the inside of Joan's head to the inside of Robert's. In real life I have only one head, one pair of eyes; one point of view. For a moment I had borrowed Joan's; I was watching the scene, as it were, over her shoulder. Now I find myself hustled to the door, so I can look over Robert's shoulder at Joan. The thread of truth is broken. I need to watch a consecutive scene over the shoulder of one character only. Let the writer switch to Robert's eye-view later on, after a break in the scene, and I have no complaint to make.

A demand that becomes more imperative with my middle years, is for good English. Not lifeless pedantry, affected polish nor even strict adherence to grammatical rules. But if, for example, I read: *How little she wanted to really expose her latent paranoia!* I am unhappy. (With the exclamation-mark, too. It makes, in prose, a writer's comment and a thrusting, tiresome one at that. The empha-

38

sis, the 'Well, fancy!' should come from me, the reader.)

I have said I want to believe the makebelieve. Just so long as I am reading. If the illusion is preserved to the last page, then the writer has done his work. Thinking over the book afterwards, I may decide that I no longer believe a word of it, that I have been kept under a temporary spell whose magic has worn off. I would still recommend the novel. Naturally, the longer its look and feel of truth last, the better it is. But if it lasts only its own lifetime of three hundred pages it has, to my mind, succeeded.

Characters that exist; an illusion of reality variously preserved; a story that moves, told in acceptable language. These are my aims. How do I (the guinea-pig for experiment and examination) set about achieving them?

Let us begin with the characters. And for this purpose I must take you first into a classroom.

2

The year was 1945 and the place was Cuerden Hall in Lancashire. Cuerden Hall and I were both in disguise. The mansion was acting under the name 'Post-Hostilities School of Army Education'. I was appearing as an officer in the A.T.S., one of the Instructors in English to the school.

I operated in a stripped room with long windows and a sad, gentle garden outside. The room held a half-circle of desks set at a respectful distance from my table, chair and blackboard. (Much of my spare time was spent in teaching myself to write legibly on the blackboard.) Behind their desks the class looked out at me dubiously: men and women wearing khaki; ages anywhere between twenty and forty-five. Their education and background varied; their attitude towards me was unanimous. When they signed on for the English course, they had not expected a woman-instructor. And they didn't want one. They had different ways of showing this. A blonde corporal yawned conscientiously and rhythmically, afterwards smiling at her neighbour. A sergeant chose to keep his cap on. There were the smart-alecks, the sitters-in-stupor.

(There were also those who had not signed on for the English course at all. One A.T.S. private landed at Cuerden under the impression that she was required as a blood-donor. Another came prepared for Musical Appreciation classes. The Instructor was well-advised to establish their intentions at the outset.)

This was the first course I had given, and the third day of it. They were turning into my friendly enemies.

I said to them: 'I should like you to try and imagine that you're all professional writers. Skilled, highly-paid writers. You're sitting at your desk, every one of you, in a warm comfortable study.' (A derisive groan: the room was freezing.) 'An editor has just commissioned you to write him a short story for fifty guineas.' (Another sort of groan.) 'You have a splendid desk, beautiful pens and paper, all ready. On the other hand you haven't an idea in your head. Now, where are you going to begin? What do you look for first?'

'A plot' they said in chorus.

'Are you quite sure?'

They were all quite sure.

'You wouldn't think about characters first?'

No, they wouldn't. Once they'd thought of a plot, they would think about the characters; not before.

'Are you—' I repeated—'quite sure?'

They were quite cross.

'All right. Let's prove it. We're going to make up a short story together. If I give you a plot will you provide the characters?'

They were agreeable.

'The plot' I said, 'is a simple one. A murder story. The murderer invites his two victims to dine with him. He has chosen to kill them by the rather unorthodox method of screwing the dining-room ceiling down on top of them, until they're squashed.' (Apologies to 'The Terribly Strange Bed', I said in my mind; I was shooting off the cuff; I hadn't planned this exercise in advance.) 'This means some elaborate mechanical preparations and some tricky timing. At the last minute they are saved because the floor gives way, dropping them a comparatively small distance into the cellar, out of harm's reach.'

My class accepted the plot.

'Here we go, then. Now it's up to you. Who is this man, this murderer?'

Heaven was on my side. A twinkling smart-aleck at the end of the row said 'A Civil Servant' and got an enthusiastic laugh from the Army.

I accepted the Civil Servant: 'But you must tell me all about him. Remember that when you create a character you want to know much more than you ever put on paper. He's got to be a real person in your mind: as solid as your neighbour at the next desk. What's his name? Any ideas?'

They came up with Augustus Simpkins. I wrote it on the board, with the rest of their findings.

He was a mousy little middle-aged man, with a mousy little middle-aged wife. Faithful to her? Yes. Crazy for her? No. Just putting up with her? Yes. He did his job ade-

quately but no more. He was never late for the office. He
didn't drive a car. Nor ride a motor-bicycle? Certainly not.
He liked gardening. He took his seaside holiday at the same
place every year. He was practically teetotal; a bad sailor;
he paid his bills regularly. What did he read? They didn't
know, though they assured me with some fervour that he
never read novels. Poetry? No, indeed. On we went. At the
end of a very few minutes every space on the blackboard
was full and we had a satisfactorily complete portrait of
Augustus. I called a halt.

'Now then,—is that a well-drawn character? A believa-
ble person?'

'Yes,' in chorus.

'You really think Augustus could exist?'

Defensively now, they swore he could. Didn't *I* think
so?

'Yes, I do indeed. I think you've done very well. He's
alive.'

While they relaxed and smiled upon me, I summed up
Augustus:—'A nice, timid, unimaginative, unadventurous
little fellow; fond of routine and peace; no particular discontent; no hobbies except his garden; no mechanical
knowledge, no special skill . . .' The temperature had begun to drop; they were getting it. 'And now,' I said, 'I must
ask you:—is Augustus a murderer? A methodical murderer? Could Augustus devise and make a screw-down
ceiling in order to commit this murder? And quite apart
from that point, who are his enemies? Where are his motives?'

It was Humbert Wolfe who first pointed out to me that
for good fiction one couldn't just rig up a plot and push
the characters in afterwards. The incident could only
arise from the characters themselves. Just as in life. People

made things happen; things didn't make people happen.

The Cuerden Hall episode was a deliciously simple proof of it. But the proof is always there. I have only to think 'I might set a book in that French village,' to ask myself at once 'Who are the people?'

Without some vision and apprehension of the people I should never get going at all. Where do they come from? In my experience, from anywhere, from everywhere, from nowhere. When they first walk in, they rarely have the look of people I know; they may develop fleeting likenesses; they may turn into portraits without my realising it. Or I may find one facet of a true personality suddenly showing up in an otherwise imaginary figure. This is the way with the important characters in the story.

For the minor characters, whom I deliberately 'audition' rather than find plucking my sleeve, the process is more dangerous. I am inclined to say to myself: 'What sort of a person is he? Somebody like A? No . . . Like B? No, B's all wrong. Oh . . . what about C? Yes, that's a good idea.' It may be. It is also the first step towards a libel-action, or at best the end of a beautiful friendship. Because, once I've decided that C fills the bill, I shall find it hard to refrain from giving the character C's looks, his job and his habits. Even those yellow socks he prefers may be included, without my conscious intention.

I was told when young that if I wanted to conceal a portrait drawn from life, I need only change the looks and the profession. Since there is quite a lot of a person left after that piece of plastic surgery, I pass the tip on for those who may like to try it.

My Rough, as I have indicated, is the process by which I hope to clear all ambiguous mist from the characters. They have been walking around in my mind without wholly revealing themselves. Now they must come into sharp, truthful focus.

From first to last it is less a matter of seeing them than of being them. Even at their earliest appearance they are likely to bring some physical characteristics along; and their looks—as one might say—grow on them without much assistance from me. Where I have to work hard is at fitting myself under the skin of each. The least likeable, the least important, must be studied and understood from his own point of view. Then from the other characters' point of view.

It is essential, as I told the Cuerden class, to know far more than ever goes down on paper. I need to know how the character will react to a dozen situations before I can determine his behaviour in one. My job is to know them all, to find none of them so mysterious that I cannot give reasons for what they do.

Nearly thirty years ago, my friend John van Druten wrote a murder-play called *Somebody Knows*. There was one obvious suspect, the man arrested and tried for the crime. But there were others who might well have been guilty. The accused was discharged for lack of evidence. And the mystery remained unsolved at the final curtain. I saw the opening performance of this play; despite its liveliness, its pace and power, I left the theatre feeling baffled and dissatisfied; I didn't know why. When I talked to the author on the following day, I asked him 'Which of them really did it?' 'I don't know,' said John van Druten.

'But that's ridiculous' I said rudely, 'you *must* know.'

He persisted that he had no idea; that was the way the play had come to him and he had settled for the mystery. Feeling crossly 'But it won't *do*', I ceased fire. So, in a remarkably short time, did the play. I am still convinced that

44

since he couldn't come to a decision about his own characters, the audience felt, and was, cheated.

The only other disclaimer of the kind in my experience was likewise made by a dramatist. This play too had a background of murder. I saw it twice. The first time was unreal; an amiable, trivial, elegant evening in the theatre, with some remarkably good acting. I saw it again a few months later; another actress was playing the part of the woman who had been charged with murder. I couldn't understand why all was different, all was real. The whole play had come to life for me.

Talking to the actress, I made this discovery. When she took over the part, she had said to the author: 'The woman is innocent, is she not? You mean her to have been wrongly accused?'

The author replied 'I really don't know . . . I've never made up my mind about that.'

'But look,' said the actress—'here are two separate lines that prove it. What else could these lines mean?'

Whether she convinced the author, I don't know. The author at least agreed to let her play the part on that assumption.

As a novelist, I am in the position of a stage-director with acting experience behind him. I must know how to act all the parts before I can hope to steer the cast. But no director can make an actor do what he doesn't believe. The actor must feel that the gesture or movement is true. He must understand it and be at ease with it. If not, he won't be able to do it. No director in his senses would force the issue. Nor, in my work, would I.

There is a suspicion of whimsy attaching to the theory that fictional characters have minds of their own, wills of their own. How can imaginary people, conjured by a writer, reject or refuse the writer's plan for them? The answer is simply that they can and they do. This, of course, is only one way of putting it. What the refusal really means is a certain ignorance on my part at the beginning. I have said that I don't really know these people until I have met them on paper. When they jib and reject my original scheme, they show me clearly that I was guessing at some of their actions before coming to a full understanding of their nature. (A little touch of Augustus Simpkins in the night . . .)

I may believe, as I work on the story that, come Chapter Ten, when war breaks out, James will join the Army. But James, having revealed something of his personality over nine chapters of the Rough, can confound me by looking far more like an R.A.F. type. Then he has to have his way.

Naturally, I am without a clue as to the impact of my characters on any reader. While I work I am wholly concerned with directing the cast as well as I know how: in other words to my own and the cast's satisfaction. The auditorium is empty. And it will never be filled in the sense that a theatre auditorium fills on the opening night. There is no immediate crowd-reaction to the characters in a novel. A scatter of solitary, invisible persons reading; putting down the book; taking a week or more to finish it; perhaps not finishing it at all . . . can a novelist ever tell how his children are being received and understood? No. But my obligation to myself and my work includes always a shadowy third. Particularly when I feel that I have cheated, played a false trick; when I tidy up and simplify a passage that was obscure; when I mutter aloud 'That's not right'; then I have the sense of an authority, an onlooker somewhere around. Perhaps it's one of the characters; perhaps it's only me.

Come behind the scenes. As already indicated, I like to view a consecutive scene 'over the shoulder' of one person only. Let us suppose that I have the fellow and the scene to hand.

Well, his name is John; his age is nineteen; he is a boy with adventurous instincts. His father, a North country businessman, would like to see him go for a sound, steady job. John has other ideas. His real longing is to travel, to see the world.

The scene that's coming up is John's first meeting with a middle-aged playboy, Morris Alderley, and the playboy's daughter Jane. Their car has involved itself in an accident outside John's house. This is an important scene because it will prove to be John's launching-platform for a series of adventures that take him around the world, falling in love with the daughter on the way.

All right. Off we go. John hears the crash, runs out of the gate and finds the splendid Continental Bentley in collision with the baker's van. Nobody hurt.

From here onwards, I must keep myself out. Remember, I have known Morris and Jane for weeks. I have acted both parts, living under both skins and thinking inside both heads. But John is seeing them for the very first time and it is unlikely that he'll think any of the things I think about those two. His mind won't make subtle or intuitive comments. He's not a witty person, so I mustn't put neat jokes into his mouth. His private observations will be limited, by his youth and by his natural simplicity.

In an earlier scene where I halted Morris before a looking-glass (one of the most obvious and most useful means of revealing a character's appearance) Morris him-

47

self decided that he looked like a dissolute and sentimental lion. John, however, will see only a large, rather florid chap wearing an expensive suit.

Jane's appearance too has been noted earlier; one of her more articulate friends observing that she has the head of a Raphael angel, the figure of Balmain's top model and the disposition of all three witches in Macbeth. John will see a tall, fair beautiful girl in a tantrum; he will put the tantrum down to the motor accident.

As John ran out of the gate, I, his director am offstage. You can't see me and you can't in fact see John in the round, because you are inside his head. You are John. You have a John's-eye-view and you'll be keeping that view right up till the moment when the sequence shuts off with the ending of the scene.

Of course you have certain advantages that he has not. (I am presuming now that you have come thus far in the book and found it readable.) However beguilingly I may persuade you that you're inside John's head, some of your own comments will keep coming in and extending the view. You have met Morris and Jane already. Although at the moment you are simply seeing them via John, you— like me—know far more about them than he does. Your knowledge provokes you to pity John. The poor young dope doesn't know what he's in for. Morris' lethal charm and Jane's beauty are taking him up a road that you see to be dangerous. Meanwhile, unconscious of his doom, the little victim seems, and is, as happy as a clam. You are not deceived? But if I do my job well, you will know how it feels to be deceived. You will know how it feels to be John.

Every mental comment, every thought is his, though I shall not write 'John saw', 'John thought' every time. (If

48

John were an American, I should write 'The windshield was smashed' instead of 'The windscreen was smashed' because John, inside his head, would be using the American word, not the English.) Not one phrase, even if it seems to be an impersonal statement, must express itself in any language but John's own. There are small traps waiting for me here. My own slang isn't John's slang. My memories aren't John's memories. The broken glass in the road might remind me of a crash I had in an Army car during the war; it couldn't do that for John who was a tot at the time.

This may all sound a strenuous, contrived way of presenting the John's-eye-view. In fact it happens automatically once I am under way. So automatically now that I forget I do it. My attention is called to it only when somebody who has read the book accuses me of holding John's opinions. My publisher once asked me to cut a reference to 'Millie's breathy little British voice,' as offensive to the British public; he hadn't noticed that I was looking at Millie through the eyes of a very American American. A reviewer once accused me of 'middle-class snobbery'; the scene of which she complained was written over the shoulder of a middle-class snob.

Before I leave John, I hope at least to make him come alive; as much alive on paper as he was in my head. When his scene ends, the point-of-view may shift to Morris or to Jane or to another. This shift demands a space, a halt. Even if there's no actual pause in time, even if Morris and Jane take John straight off to the local hotel for lunch while the car's being repaired, I must, if I want to move over into Morris' head, begin a new chapter; or at least divide the next scene from the last by means of a space and a Roman numeral. I have now left John.

How has he emerged from his first appearance? Is he

likeable or inimical? I don't think I can label him. I know him too well. By the end of the book I shall know them all far too well, in the process of being them, to pass judgement. Even the meanest character acquires a different perspective when one has lived inside him. From my point of view every one of the people in the book is a real human being: a mixture, therefore, of good and bad; sometimes sympathetic to me, sometimes detestable.

I care about them all. If I didn't, I shouldn't have written their story. But when the question of whether I *meant* a certain character to be 'unsympathetic' was fired at me by an American publisher, I could only reply that she had her good side and her bad side. 'Are we meant to be rooting for her?' came next. I couldn't answer that one to the publisher's satisfaction.

All I know is that to try to slant a character for sympathy, to aim at satisfying the 'rooting' instinct, is something I cannot, will not and dare not do. If the invaders of my head emerge finally as a bunch of stinkers, it isn't my affair. I've told their truth and my own to the best of my ability.

Nobody, as Virginia Woolf points out, has ever known just why a character should be 'convincing' for one reader and shadowy for another. We have never discovered just what magic it is that makes a fictional being put on flesh and blood for us when we meet him.

Does my John's-eye-view method inevitably give him his best chance of coming alive? It must be decided, I think, by the character's relationship with the other people in the book. Sometimes I have found it absolutely necessary to keep out of a character's head; to present him only as he appears to the others.

I did this in a novel called *The Willow Cabin*. The man

was named Michael Knowle. Michael was a man with a secret. He died, as he had lived, with the secret still kept. Throughout the story, many people looked at Michael and drew their different conclusions. He was the target for several contradictory theories. Should you chance to read the book, you will find that there is no Michael's-eye-view anywhere.

As a mystery-man he could never, it seemed to me, reveal himself. Certainly I lived inside Michael's head, was Michael, knew Michael as well as I knew the others. But in honesty I couldn't write from his angle and still suppress the most important matter in his thoughts. It would have felt like cheating. And I doubt he would have come alive that way.

Since this was a book that sold well, I did hear some readers' reactions to Michael. The majority disliked him. All were inclined to sit in judgement on his behaviour. My guess is that the reaction came from missing his point-of-view on the whole issue. There were others in the book who behaved, from time to time, worse than Michael ever behaved. But I had given these a chance to speak for themselves, to reveal their motives.

Wouldn't a character get the best chance of all, then, if I let him tell his story in the First Person? First Person Singular still beckons me every time there's a novel on the way. It is a direct and lively method. It carries, or should, a truthful ring from the moment the teller of the tale opens his mouth.

It has other advantages. Where the words themselves are concerned, they tend to flow more easily; as though one were writing a letter. The 'I' allows a greater liberty in the use of colloquial speech. And there is no struggle to shift the point-of-view. Here is one point of view, one single set of opinions; one series of snapshots taken with the camera-lenses of one pair of eyes. Surely all this must combine to produce a vivid, vital unity?

Well, yes and no. The style is, I think, the main advantage. I have only to read in a review the words 'beautifully written' to guess with almost invariable accuracy that this novel is written in the First Person Singular. The unity is certainly made to one's hand. Many scenes will benefit. Much will be vivid, shareable, understandable.

But the method demands particular skill. It has its own hazards. The first difficulty, to my mind, is in the presentation of the character himself. Too often he sounds like myself talking; my own thoughts and phrases thin him down. I am more often hearing him than seeing or being him. The repeated 'I' makes him, unjustly, an egoist. He sounds pleased with himself when he isn't. He can acquire a kind of strut. Involved in a love-affair, both the male and the female 'I' incline to turn tedious. They strike the note struck by the friend sitting opposite you, hopelessly in love, 'telling you all about it' and in the process, sounding much like every ego-bound lover since the beginning of time.

Remember also, how greatly I am limiting the focus and scope of the scenes themselves. This 'I' must be at the heart of the action all the while; or else I must find deft ways of bringing him up to date with what he's missed. (He wasn't there . . . he couldn't have been there . . . how does he know what went on? How can I show that X hates him when *he* doesn't know it and X wouldn't dream of telling him to his face? I want A's slant on all this; how to get it—when the whole story is told with 'I's' slant, and A and 'I' never meet?)

An eccentric character is, I think, the easiest to trust with the telling of his own story. Or a horror without self-

52

knowledge, drawing his own unconsciously satiric portrait as he goes. But as I confine myself to the limits of one person's experience, so I am likely to meet with some heavy going.

Which isn't to say that this method hasn't succeeded brilliantly in the past, and still succeeds. In contemporary fiction I think first of J. D. Salinger's Holden Caulfield, next of Ian Jefferies' John Craig. Both are odd, arresting, three-dimensional customers. The most teasing 'I' lives in my favourite novel of the last ten years, Rose Macaulay's *Towers of Trebizond*. This character, Laurie, I assumed to be a young man (just as the author apparently meant me to do) instead of a young woman. With the result that I accepted—among other things—what seemed a most adult, truthful and nonchalant approach to a homosexual love-affair. Not for months did I find I was wrong. When I did, I re-read the book. The devices to conceal the sex of Laurie are endless; there are only four straight clues.

Of the minor characters, somebody told me once 'There's no such thing as a minor character' and thereby frightened me to death. Since then I have made every effort to keep them vividly in view, to treat them respectfully and not dress them out of the acting-box. They are difficult to 'wind off'. This winding-off process happens naturally to the bigger fish. Their onward movement is what they themselves have willed in the beginning, is the fabric of the novel itself. Whatever their fate, they will have started out from point 'A' and got to point 'Z'.

The minor characters have not this journey in their nature; they merely dart in and out of the scene. Yet it is essential that they should somehow manage to make a complete statement of themselves within their small scope.

53

None of them should leave a vague impression behind. (Not even those who *are* vague? No. There should be a clear impression of vagueness.)

And their looks? How do I, our guinea-pig, solve this question of pinning on paper the physical image I have in my mind? I have already given one glimpse in my dealings with Jane and Morris. As a reader I don't want too detailed a description of a character's appearance. I want an impression. No catalogue of features and colouring can give a lifelike impression; one doesn't, in real life, measure the proportions of a face; one's eyes don't immediately, take a thoughtful Kodacolor snapshot.

An author whose work I admire profoundly, once wore out my powers of admiration and reception with his long, detailed examination of the leading character's looks at the opening of his first chapter. I ended up with no picture at all.

In life, the picture at first glance may consist of a blue rinse, a smile, crowsfeet and earrings. I try to give this kind of sketch; which is not to say that I succeed. Among the pitfalls are the automatic needs to revive the sketch at intervals when the character is on stage. Repetition of physical characteristics *ad nauseam* is one of the habits I have to watch. Repetition of characteristic phrases, too: see the *New Yorker* column called 'Infatuation-With-Sound-Of-Own-Words Department.' The characters' tricks of speech also tend to borrow from my own and it's all right if just one talks as I do, all wrong if even two speak with the same voice.

Before I go further into the matter of dialogue (a vital tool in the work of bringing these people to life) I must briefly explore another character-mystery.

54

3

'You're *analysing me!* You're going to put Nicholas and me in a book!'

This affrighted shout went up in the middle of Stewart's tea-room, on the corner of Old Bond Street. The year was 1928. My former school-friend was telling me the story of how she had become engaged to a young man on her recent journey to Canada. I, who longed for a love-affair, was sitting in a happy cloud of vicarious romance. I wasn't analysing anything. I was just having a good time; as when I sat in the dress-circle at the Haymarket: well, perhaps not quite as good a time as that, but pretty enjoyable all the same. I only wanted more.

'Go *on*,' I begged. 'I swear I won't put it in a book.'

She shut up like a box. She said it would all go into my next novel.

Rapidly I lost my temper. I said that she was nice, that Nicholas was obviously *very* nice, and they were going to be married which was *jolly* nice. But couldn't she see that such a nice straightforward story, beginning when they met on a skating-rink in Montreal, and ending with the diamond half-hoop that she was flashing at me across the table, couldn't possibly make a novel?

She didn't believe me.

Since then my voyagings have brought me many discoveries about nice characters. One discovery was crystallised by an observation of Lettice Cooper's when we were on a platform together. The audience was bemoaning the fact that novelists always wrote about such disagreeable people. (It is an old moan; I first heard it raised when I was twenty.) This time they were unanimous and very vocal. Why did they never meet, in the modern novel, any counterpart of themselves or their friends?

'What,' whispered Lettice Cooper in my ear, 'makes them think *they're* all so nice?' This gave me not only giggles but the instant craving to follow all the believers-in-their-own-niceness home into their private lives and see what cooked.

The virtues I admire in life can bore me to death in a contemporary novel: whether I am reading this novel or writing it. *The greatest of these is charity* . . . Yes, indeed and indeed; nobody in his senses would argue with that one. But the portrait of a thoroughly charitable person on paper can be so much porridge. Ten to one, full-scale nobility emerges as an infuriator. I don't believe I have ever found a successful study of a saint in fiction. Saints come out as stuffed hair-shirts.

The lifelong battle between good and evil in the human soul makes a huge, heroic story. But my pen inclines to approach it obliquely, specially, taking as small a corner of the immense panorama as it can.

When an audience clamours for 'nice people', I wonder what they mean—or think they mean? Unaware of themselves below the surface, do they want a painless tale that presents a series of surfaces, all looking perfectly fine? Would they like it, should they read it? 'If what you are after is sinless literature, what you will get is no literature,' said a Cardinal. Speaking for myself, nothing could make me feel less cosy than a cosy approach to life shown by the author and the characters in a novel. It discomforts me not because it fails to make any record of tragedy, but because it implies that there is none to record.

Yet the characters who are all failures, all apparently in

love with their own failure, the listless, mixed-up despairers, the fashion of these days, arouse the Colonel with the white moustache who lives inside me (along with a rebel and a rabbit and a mort of contradictory types). The Colonel doesn't want them to be nice, dammit; he wants to see a few guts around here.

4

Back to dialogue.

My first precaution is never to let a line of it stay on paper unless I have read it aloud. This is the only way, I think, to learn to write good dialogue. What do I mean by 'good'?

I mean that it must ring true upon the ear. Whether its function be to reveal character, to advance the action or to create an atmosphere, it must sound as though it had been spoken naturally by a living person. Obviously the effect of 'natural' dialogue is something of an illusion, a conjuring-trick. People in novels must talk more pointedly and tidily than in real life. Some of the cackle must be cut.

Euphony, vital in any narrative or descriptive passage, is less of a problem while the characters are talking. Even so, the phrase: 'Isn't that shellac too black, Jack?' reminds me again how much of my reading is done with my ears.

A heavy hand with the spoken word is like a heavy hand with pastry. However good the ingredients—the subject-matter, the argument—heavy-handedness can wreck the finished product. ('Ah, Charles, how subtly every emotion of yours contrives to offset and enhance every emotion of mine,' exclaimed Elizabeth . . .)

A watch must be kept on the 'Said-George-Said-Mabel'

frame in which the talk conducts itself. For me 'Said' is good enough. Better than its unrewarding alternatives: Exclaimed; remarked; declared; stated; observed; expostulated; commented; opined. Occasionally one of these may prove useful, but for the donkey-work give me dear old Said every time. It has the advantage of being unobtrusive when you want it to be. It can be effective in its own right: even capable of adding drama. How? Here are two people approaching a dark, motionless object lying at the foot of the cellar steps.

'Hold it! Stay where you are . . .'

'What's wrong, darling?'

'Something lying here. Wait.'

'I'll put the light on.'

'No . . . don't. Not for a minute, please.'

'Why on earth not?'

'Listen, Margaret. I want you to do as I tell you. Don't put any lights on. Go straight back into the kitchen and wait for me.'

'George, you're frightening me. What is it? What's *down* there, for Heaven's sake?'

'Reuben's body' said George.

You will notice that each addresses the other by name as the serious moment comes. That is the reflection, in my experience, of a human habit at serious moments. If, however, I halt them in the kitchen to take a stiff drink and consider the next move, I shall be making a mistake to let the dialogue go this way:—

'George . . . *how* could it happen?'

'I don't know, Margaret.'

'Reuben was such a sweet person, George. Why should anyone want to kill him?'

58

'Look, Margaret, that's what we have to find out. But the first thing we do is call the police.'

'George . . . must we?'

'Yes, Margaret.'

Had enough?

The inexperienced writer holds one of two views about dialogue. (a) He has a natural gift for it ('My friends all say I ought to write a play') in which case he will use it by the yard when it isn't needed. (b) It frightens him into heavy-handedness. This is the worse predicament; he will overload; he will plug in an adverb by way of a short cut; and the result will be rather like this:—

'But I say, talking of Reuben's death,' Josephine interrupted excitedly, 'has anybody remembered that *on* Friday afternoon, Henrietta and Ludovic were meeting him at the empty house next door at six to discuss the decorations?'

All the above facts have come down on paper already. Every character present knows:

(a) That Reuben is dead. (In which case 'talking of Reuben's death' is not only unnatural, but unnecessary.)

(b) That he was to meet Ludovic and Henrietta on Friday evening, for the purpose stated.

(c) That the house next door is empty.

The reader knows all this too. The writer is merely rounding up some evidence in a hurry, using the clumsiest sort of dialogue as vehicle for its presentation and writing the adverb 'excitedly' because he can't be bothered with any other method of showing us that Josephine was excited.

Let us see if we can do better:—

"Josephine's hand shook, tilting the sherry in her glass.

59

Her voice was taut, unsteady: 'Reuben was with Henrietta and Ludovic next door at six o'clock—remember?' "

I am vowed to the preservation of urgency and immediacy in a scene of this sort. I am also vowed to an honest picture of it *as it plays between the characters*. This picture must never be sacrificed for the sake of jogging my own memory. Least of all with dialogue must I allow unwieldy stretches of information to come in.

What have I got against the adverb 'excitedly'? Only its failure to 'show'. It simply tells. It was in the classroom at Cuerden that I gave the exercise of substituting an action for an adverb.

1. Gloomily.

George tramped to the window and stood there, looking out, his head lowered, his shoulders hunched. He did not speak.

2. Gaily.

Josephine laughed, wrinkled her nose at him and danced towards the telephone.

3. Pompously.

Ludovic rose to his feet, pulled down his waistcoat, adjusted his features and began to intone.

Doesn't the adverb, as they used to ask me in class, make for a quicker pace? Well, no; not necessarily. It may make the scene *shorter*, but this is by no means the secret of pace.

My reason for eyeing the adverb warily (and it can be a most useful creature on occasion) is my confirmed preference for taking pictures; snapshots of the characters whenever possible; talking-pictures as the dialogue runs. It is one of the ways I work towards 'the illusion of reality, variously preserved', my demand as a reader.

CHAPTER
TWO

My next demand, you may remember, is for a story that moves, taking me along with it; a condition of things that unfolds and reveals, by way of a beginning, a middle and an end.

Back for a moment, to the Cuerden Hall classroom. When I gave the lesson in Narrative Writing I stuck to the War Office syllabus, seldom introducing variations of my own.

The exercise began with my reading to them the parable of the Good Samaritan. Like many of the parables, it is written almost entirely in nouns and verbs; there's no adjectival nor adverbial embroidery. I would ask the class to see what they could do in the same manner. They were asked to record the journey from their units to Cuerden Hall. No descriptive touches allowed; unless these could be given by verbs and nouns.

After a few minutes I would call the exercises in and read some of their beginnings aloud. They packed a punch and they had a look of style. They were like hot-rods stripped down. The verbs, the wheels, moved them along. The phrase: 'I went out of the gate and down the road to the station' cannot help having movement in it. Always, my mixed bag of students agreed that if they picked up a magazine and began to read a story that opened like this, they would want to go on.

'But supposing,' I said, 'I'd given you all time to finish the exercise, if in fact you'd ended with your arrival here, would that have been enough to make a short story?'

They were quick in saying No; quick in coming up with the need for our old friend the plot.

'What is a plot?'

'Begins with a character, Ma'am,' somebody would tell me, dutifully recalling Augustus Simpkins.

'But what *is* it? There's no trap here. I'm asking you to solve a problem of definition. I've never yet solved it myself.'

They were as dissatisfied as I with the old answer: 'Boy meets girl; boy loses girl; boy gets girl', their most usual complaint being that it didn't say how. They would dodge all around the problem, without arriving at a definition. A plot, they said, involved 'things happening', 'unexpected twists', 'suspense'. Here I would suggest the word 'conflict'. A moment of happy relaxation was inevitably followed by somebody asking me what I meant by Conflict?

I said 'A man trying to walk through a locked door.'

I don't remember how my fellow-instructors in the English Wing fared with this one. I do remember that my students were baffled. Almost as baffled as when, in the Descriptive Writing lesson, I asked them to describe a wheelbarrow for the benefit of somebody who had never used nor seen one. (For the first step towards a nervous breakdown, I can cordially recommend this exercise.) After much musing, we would eventually decide that a plot was a linked series of actions and reactions; that its pattern of stresses must provide a beginning, a middle and an end. (I am inclined to think I was calling the tune. The auxiliary who defined a plot as 'the thing that keeps you reading' probably said it all.)

A Beginning . . . While a novel is still at its early, dreaming stage in my head, I am by no means sure where it will begin. There is a searchlight swinging to and fro, disclosing the lives of these people in sharp, intermittent glimpses. Sometimes it will reveal facts with which, I think, I need have no particular concern. These are things I should know, not necessarily things I must tell. They will remain below the surface, surely, as for iceberg. Not always; most disconcertingly, they can insist on making themselves a visible part of the story. The process, in my solitary monologue, goes like this:—

'That's what happened, of course, but it isn't necessary to the narrative.'

'Oh yes it is.'

'But look, it all happened years ago . . . it's ten years behind the rest of the action.'

'Too bad.'

'But I can't possibly fit it in.'

'You'll have to.'

The stern, Nanny-ish monitor is suddenly replaced by one of my more persistent devils, chirping 'How about a flashback?' He knows I am pliable here. I fell in love with the flashback method when I was nineteen, and for years I believed that any story was the better for having bitten its tail, like a fried whiting. You know what I mean. Time, the present: two old ladies talking as they look at a faded photograph. Dissolve to time-the-past, with the old ladies as young girls, the man in the photograph alive and desirable. Proceed through the love-story, dissolve to the present again, and there are the old ladies with the faded photograph. 'We both loved him, in our different ways . . . A cup of tea, dear?'

Over the years I have come to admit, slowly, reluctantly, that a story should begin at the beginning and end at the end. But the lure of a flashback *anywhere* in a novel is still strong. So I glower at the devil and am wondering whether to yield when another devil snaps 'Prologue?'

'Prologue . . .' I see what he means. Enclose the ten-years-before situation in a prologue and then cut to Chapter One. Legitimate, but if this solution is recorded in the notebook, I am liable to find 'WHY DON'T I LIKE THAT?' written immediately below: last reflection before leaving the desk and sulking my way into real life again.

I remember this situation arising with acute ferocity when I was, I thought, almost ready to begin writing my novel *Ask Me No More*. The story was set in the nineteen-fifties. The protagonists were two middle-aged women. They had (like the dear old ladies conning the faded photograph) loved the same man. He died years before my story opened. One woman had married him. The other had borne a child by him. The child, now growing up, was to become the cause of battle between the two women. I could see the progress of the battle, right up to the end.

But the searchlight was swinging, to illuminate the past. So it should, I thought. I wanted to see the dead man, the old love-affair, the beginning of it all.

I began to know what had happened in 1938. The searchlight swung obligingly until I knew enough. It must, I agreed with my devil, be indicated somewhere in flashback: a glimpse of the fatal encounter that had provoked and determined Today. Just an episode recalled . . .

The episode went on recalling itself. In detail. 'Stop,

can't you?' I said to the searchlight. But its beam swung in a wider arc; its illumination wouldn't stop. Here were the women in their twenties, the dead man brought back to life again, the beginning as it was. Flashback? No flashback could possibly accommodate the vivid, truculent series of scenes as they played themselves through in my head.

I must begin the book, I realised miserably, in 1938 instead of 1957. I struggled a little while, this way, with the Nanny-ish monitor:

'Oh *no.*'

'*Oh yes.*'

''Mean—tell it all straight, as it happened?'

'*Of course.*'

'I can't.'

'*You will.*'

'Well, but after 1938, what? *Not* the war, I beg you.'

'*The war.*'

'Hell's teeth . . .'

'*You know what happened to them in the war.*'

'Well, of course I do. But I didn't expect to have to live it through on paper. It was to come out in back-references, —short ones—done in the dialogue.'

'*Well it isn't; not any more.*'

'Oh, honestly . . . 1938 will run to about a third of the book; then the war-years . . . Here's my whole original novel, complete in itself, doing no harm to anyone, almost ready to write—turning into what?'

'*Into Book Three.*'

'Book Three . . . So it is. Isn't that fine? How long before I catch up with my proposed first chapter, I ask myself?'

'*About six months.*'

Six months it was.

I suppose I could have fought harder to preserve the original shape and the alluring flashback. But experience has taught me to beware of taking an obstinate stand in the early stages: to await the true beginning, however brutally its authentic appearance may bulldoze my plans.

A Middle . . . What is the middle of a novel? This, surely, should be a mere matter of arithmetic. Three hundred pages of print: turn back to page 150: obvious, isn't it? Well, no. At least it's not what I mean by the middle. The middle might come before page 150, or after it. The middle might consist of thirty pages or three. I have a clear picture of the middle in my mind, or rather, two clear pictures. The first is a watershed; the Great Divide, if you like; the point where the rivers begin to flow West into the Pacific instead of East into the Atlantic. The other picture is the cross-tide in shallow water where two currents meet, curling up and over in a small, angry wave. That's the middle. Here comes, or should come, the moment when impulse and action drive together, making a peak from which the story flows on inevitably to its end. And having said that, I'm aware that I have said nothing. I must illustrate, using myself as guinea-pig for the experiment again.

The novel I choose is called *The Bridge*. Number of pages, in the English edition, 299. The Middle begins at page 139 and runs to page 154.

The Bridge is the tale of a soul's journey through Purgatory. On the journey, the soul of the dead man David Neilson meets, re-lives and resolves the sins of his past life that bar his way to Paradise. At first he moves like an automaton, without conscious memory. He encounters his past selves, (a boy, a young man, a soldier), selves whom at first he scarcely recognises, judging their actions as though

66

they were strangers to him. Gradually the soul develops a memory; acquaints itself again with its life on earth and owns to it. Now its judgement becomes more severe.

When the soul of Neilson has re-lived the episode by which Neilson in life was responsible for his own daughter's death, the middle of the book has been reached. The scene on earth shows how all Neilson's weaknesses had contributed to the one fatal, foolish little gesture that helped the girl to die. The scene played in the Purgatorial courtroom shows Neilson on trial at the bar of his own remorse. From that point in life, Neilson moved on inevitably towards his own appointment with death. From that point in Purgatory, where the soul smashed its self-appointed prison, the end of the journey to Paradise came in sight.

An End . . . I have seldom heard anyone say of a novel he has enjoyed, 'The end is perfect.' On the contrary. Nearly always I am told 'You'll find the ending rather weak': 'The end's *wrong*, somehow': 'It has a disappointing end.' My suspicion is that nobody likes coming to the end of a book he has enjoyed; therefore he grumbles automatically at the way of it.

As far as my work is concerned, there can never be much argument in my mind about the end. This dictates itself before I get to the Rough; it is the belay to which I fasten that first tentative rope. Of all the matters that plan themselves ahead, this is the least likely to change. Looking back, I cannot remember a time when it changed. Except in the case of my first published novel. Here (at the age of eighteen) I was all set to kill off the man and send the woman into sad, wise widowhood. I was just about to write this last, marvellously miserable chapter when I mentioned it to Edgar Wallace, who blinked at me and said, 'Why?'

There was really no answer, except I wanted it that way. 'Doesn't solve anything, does it?' Edgar Wallace asked. 'As far as I can see, you've got two people with something to say to each other. If he dies, it doesn't get said. If you keep him alive, they can say it.'

'And then live happily ever after?'

'Anything wrong with that? Besides, you can't tell, can you?—unless you're going to write a sequel. You just leave them reunited.'

It was good advice, like all the advice Edgar Wallace gave me during the brief and valued time I knew him. But not even he, the master storyteller, could teach me, in those days, how to tell a story. Storytelling seemed to the child of eighteen an obsolete device. She liked her crackly, wispy little pictures of love with a dash of fantasy; modelled for the most part on Michael Arlen. Love was the only thing worth writing about. Sex was the only adventure (possibly because she had not experienced it.) But a story . . . goodness, what an old-fashioned notion.

Times have changed. And in my present aim to tell a story, to make what may be a good story better, I become more aware of the need for pace. It is, in some ways, a puzzle. When I said that shortening a sentence didn't necessarily make for speed, I was expounding a part of the puzzle.

The novelist has the tools of speed made to his hand. He can do in three words what the dramatist cannot do without the assistance of set-designer, carpenter, crew and a fifteen-minute interval. His 'curtain' comes down in a moonlit garden; it can rise inside the house by the use of three words: 'In her bedroom'. It can rise anywhere he likes. He can take a six-thousand mile journey between the ending of Chapter Two and Chapter Three. 'From his window, Richard watched the fog rolling in across the Golden Gate.' Here we all are, then, in San Francisco. No trouble.

Over the years I have learned that every scene has a natural end to it; when the end comes, I must guard against elaboration, against an artificial wind-off. There needs no thunderous chord struck, no pointed little comment. ('And he strode from the room.') The curtain can come down on a spoken question that doesn't get an answer. I can, if I have done right by the scene, leave them all standing just where they are. In the shifting of the scene, pace is essential—and easy, once you learn that you can get them upstairs without mentioning the stairs.

But there is, of course, far more to learn than that. The true mastery of pace comes only with hard work and long experience. It is part of the fabric, and there are no simple rules applicable to any and every novel. My own danger-signal, when the pace begins to sag, is my own dullness of spirit, a faint boredom coming up on the air as I write.

Time to stop and think. Is this scene really necessary at all? Was I wrong when I assumed it to be vital? That takes me back to the beginning; I can nearly always trace a serious fault to the foundations rather than to the structure. Was the original plan a mistake, after all?

My aim was to include—let us say—a faithful picture of how they all managed to keep going after Dad, having left his job, walked out on the family, taking the Post Office Savings account. Well now, Dad is my central character and I am concerned primarily with the way he managed to patent his invention of a soundless electric drill. Am I then, concentrating too much on background-scenes at the expense of the main story? Dad's my boy. Do I really need to live for a while with Mum in the deserted house at Stoke-on-Trent?

69

I have decided I do; that for the truthful purpose of the story I must take in Mum's despair as well as Dad's crusade. All right. Still I must heckle myself further: Do I need more than a snapshot of Mum in an atmospheric, descriptive setting? If that's all, then I can contain my purpose within a short single scene, provided I light up, either in thought or dialogue, the passage of time that has gone before:

'Molly Lawes looked at the "Feathered Friends" calendar hanging above the dresser. March the Twenty-Fourth. Sixteen days now since she had heard the front door slam, heard the sound of his footsteps going away down the street.'

The loneliness of the house, the money running low, the children's questions, the neighbours' prying assaults: every aspect of her dilemma can show itself vividly in one panel of thought. My secondary aim, to mark the passage of time, is already half achieved. A wind-off can help me achieve it altogether: 'Tomorrow, she knew, would be like today, only worse.'

However, I am not out of the wood yet. The problem may be trickier than that. The unsatisfactory sagging and the slowness may have descended upon some forward movement in the action; an event that should be swift, disturbing and alive. It might be Mum's discovery that the eldest daughter Rosamund has seized the opportunity of Dad's departure to marry her Jamaican boy-friend secretly. I was looking forward to this bit. Now it's just a great big bore. Why?

My first precaution is to take another look at the angle from which I'm writing the scene. This could well be the trouble. There's nothing that can freshen up the matter so quickly as a new point of view. I may be tired of watching the proceedings over the shoulder of despairing Mum. I could, instead, take Rosamund's-eye-view; or the Jamaican's; or perhaps make a journey into the head of the priest who married them. Or I could turn myself temporarily into that busybody neighbour who got the story first. I have freedom of choice. A thing has to happen. I can show it happening any way I like. Once it has happened, I am concerned (in this case) with the breaking of the news to Mum and with Mum's reaction. This latter scene can start right up in the middle. It needs no beginning. I don't need to break the news twice, unless I want to. Mum reels back, into the space by the wall where the television-set stood before it was removed on account of the unpaid instalments. She takes one glance at the two smiling faces, the white and the dark. (It's now obvious which cat is out of what bag.) The happy tears come to her eyes; she holds out her arms to them both. (Yes, I know; you thought she was going to be furious.)

The pace has improved. I couldn't have done the story the same service by cutting. Cutting is a matter for serious deliberation, not smart obedience to the editor. (This figure, particularly in American publishing-houses, creates a problem. Beware the editor when he declares that 'All this can come right out.' In one historic experience of my own, he was cutting the answer to a mystery that had been running through three quarters of the book.)

My own rule is never to start cutting and trimming until I have finished the job. It is, I believe, a sound rule. The writer of a first thriller showed me the work in progress not long ago. It wasn't yet done. The rough typescript was getting what looked to be severe treatment when I came into the room.

'I've been all day trying to see where I can cut,' said

the writer,—'You see, at this rate, it's going to be about ten thousand words too long.'

'How do you know?'

'Robert says 80,000 words is the right length for a whodunit.'

No offence to Robert, an intelligent young man in the publishing-business, but my blood-pressure rose immediately.

'That's just the sort of information you don't need at the minute,' I snapped.

'Why not? He knows what he's talking about. I thought if I cut from—'

—'Oh for heaven's sake, get to the end, write your story, keep it alive. *Don't* stop off to do instructed surgical operations at this stage. How many times have I told you not to listen to anybody—'

—'Except you,' said the writer, with some justification.

Cutting the dead wood, the unnecessary junk and clutter, is always helpful to the story. But it must be decided after due consideration, and it must never be done in a hurry. The smallest cut can wreck the balance of a scene, the cadence of a paragraph. When I begin on cuts, I know I must be prepared also for considerable re-assessment and revision.

I know also that one fatal slower of the pace can be found in the adjectives. I don't mean in a long string of unnecessary adjectives that hold up the action. I mean adjectives that say precisely nothing and so make time hang heavy. The colourless phrase, the phrase that gives no picture, brings a sag of its own. Take a look at the adjective, and see why.

1. *They ate well and drank an excellent hock with the meal.*

2. *It was a quaint old cottage.*

3. *After an uneventful drive they reached Kidderminster.*

4. *The band was playing a nostalgic waltz.*

5. *She wore a smart coat and skirt.*

1. *'They ate well and drank an excellent hock with the meal.'*

What's wrong with that? The hock *was* excellent and they *were* eating a meal. Weren't they? Yes. But is there any need to be quite so drearily, perfunctorily informative? Here are two flesh-and-blood characters eating and drinking. The dull little reporter's phrase has drained the life out of them. If there's no need to include the comment, the comment can go. If, on the other hand, some description of the event is wanted, the writer must think about it and think truthfully. His characters are more likely to come up with the truth than he is. This way:

Should the host know about wine, he will know the name and the vintage of this hock. He may indeed, like most people who know about wine, treat the subject with a certain pomposity. On the other hand he may be a young man without a clue, in which case he'll consult the waiter. Perhaps the girl with him hasn't a clue; even so, she can think that the wine tastes of flowers; she can still like the look of it in the long-stemmed glass. And incidentally, nobody eating a meal thinks of it as 'the meal'. Potted shrimps? Steak? What? Here I am interrupted by the writer arguing plaintively, 'Yes, but I want to get *on;* I don't want to go into these details. I simply want to say, without lingering, that they ate hearty and drank well.'

In that case, sir, a two-line snapshot of the host adding up the bill would be a considerable improvement on your first thought. Even 'Whacko, what a dinner,' from the girl as they walk out has a little vulgar life in it.

2. *'It was a quaint old cottage.'*

It was, was it? In what way? What was quaint about this cottage? Thatch? Chimneys? Sanitation? I'm sorry, but I have no picture and although I don't need a house-agent's advertisement, I'm bogged down. Low roof, crumbling red brick—any impression of shape and colour, will get me going. 'But I don't,' retorts the writer, 'want to waste my time giving you an impression.' Well, sir, I'm afraid you're wasting mine when you ask me to take your word for it that this cottage was quaint.

3. *'After an uneventful drive, they reached Kidderminster.'*

What's wrong with that? ('It's what I *mean*, and the things that happen in Kidderminster are important. I'm merely getting you there.')

Are you? Look at your statement again. If you mean that there was no accident, no delaying fog-patch or thunderstorm, no wrong turning taken and the baby wasn't sick, it was indeed an uneventful drive. But you have yet to catch my attention. You are pointing at a dull journey as though I should take note of it. You're not getting me there; you're holding me up. Why?

Should you mean to stress the uneventfulness, one of your characters might observe that this was the first time the Kidderminster road was navigated without disaster. But if you are, in truth, merely skipping the journey (which looks to me eminently worth skipping) then skip it with honesty. Cut it. Ring up your curtain in Kidderminster; pouring rain, the house with the green gate, and *whose* is the malevolent face glimpsed at the window? . . . or what you will.

4. *'The band was playing a nostalgic waltz.'*

74

Certainly bands do this. But the laziness of the adjective has made me, the reader, lazy too. Couldn't you at least come clean with the Blue Danube? If one of the characters is taken with a particular nostalgia (as surely one of them must be; nostalgia not being a quality apprehended by all present, like smell or noise . . .) may I not have it put to me plainly, vividly? 'The hackneyed, beloved "Blue Danube" reminded Albertine of her last dance with Rudolph.'
5. *'She wore a smart coat and skirt.'*

You have my sympathy: clothes are maddening things to describe. But 'smart' won't do, I fear. It's a common little word in that context, a shop-window word, a spring-catalogue word, and if we are by any chance thinking that 'chic' would be better, we had better think again. Colour? Lines? Tweed? Flannel? Quite a bore, is it not? Wiser perhaps to settle for colour alone; then to let one of the characters looking at this forty-guinea masterpiece give a whoop of appreciation. Or, more credibly, a wail: *'Why* can I never find a suit like that?' The impression of a spectacularly well-dressed woman can be recorded via the envious thoughts of others. If nobody's there but the wearer herself, she can take to the looking-glass; thinking, as she looks, how right she was, how well it fits, how much better the black than the bottle-green, her first choice.

Any impression, any visual picture, however brief, has a vividness that helps the pace. To speed matters up by using two lines instead of one: well, here I am back at the puzzle; unless I adapt my Cuerden pupil's line and conclude that 'pace is the thing that keeps you reading.'

With the above examples, I have of course been exploiting my need to be shown rather than told. And you can try to confound me, if you will, by reminding me of my own method with the John's-eye-view. Might not a drab, adjectival comment be fairly made when the scene is observed through the eyes of a colourless, unimaginative person? Might not such a person *think* 'an excellent hock', 'a quaint old cottage' and such?

No; I don't believe that anybody, however unimaginative, *thinks* that way. He may, when he speaks, express himself like that, but there are sharper, truer images in his mind than he can ever put into words. And when, as a writer, I am living under his skin, I should be truthful to his inner vision. He may see abstract affairs like that:— the Government, the Foreigners, the Cost of Living; but when he sees something at close range, his thoughts will be vivid, personal, his own eyes taking their own picture. My task is to record the taking of that picture.

Thus, I would not write 'The death of a distant relative some years before had left her with a small independent income.' To read this might not worry you; it might tell you all you need to know. You could perhaps go happily on from there. But if I wrote it I should hear the note of my own voice fatally sounding. I should also feel horribly remote from this character. I am not, with this kind of phrase, doing what I always need to do:—'pull the action nearer'; take close-ups of the close-ups. This character may well be a drab little woman whose point-of-view doesn't seem important. I should still make her turn on her heel, as it were, and look at her situation through her own eyes, using her own thoughts.

(She wouldn't think 'a distant relative'; she would think of the person by name; she wouldn't think 'some years before'; she would remember the date. She might *say* 'a small independent income', but she would *think* '£350 a year.')

But (you may reply) doesn't the word 'narrative', with

76

which I began this chapter, *mean* telling? If my demand, as a reader, is for a story that moves, if that's what I'm after when I sit down to write, then why must I be so pernickety? Must we have all this fuss about the words?

Well, I did say 'told in acceptable language . . .'

CHAPTER
THREE

1

'You want to be easy with the words and the words will be easy with you,' said George Moore. Here I find a hint of my own belief in the Great Relax instead of the Great Fuss; though I am not entirely sure I know what he means.

Am I, I ask myself, 'being easier' with the words than when I first began to write? I can recall my early passion for putting phrases back to front:—'Cold, it was'; 'Brooded the little white Georgian houses.' (Even if they did, which I doubt, it would have been easier to convey my meaning with the verb at the end of the sentence.) I think that was the Michael Arlen influence, soon sent packing by Edgar Wallace. Sometimes I was up to deliberate tricks; sometimes I wrote elaborately because I hadn't learned to express myself simply. Nobody who published three novels and a book of short stories between the ages of nineteen and twenty-one, can revisit them at fifty-two without an 'Ouch'; so I will not take them from the shelf now; but I think I can remember enough.

At twenty-three, the score was five novels and two books of short stories. By that time, my style was going through a brief phase of improvement. Looking back, I am not sure how it came. (Through hard work? Through the concussion of first love? Through leaving home, knowing guilt and grief and worry? Through taking a job in advertising as a copywriter? Through making Rebecca West my literary idol and a well-chosen idol, too . . .) Well, even if I can't determine exactly how the improvement came, I know all too well how it went.

The sixth novel, published in 1932, marked a move-on. I am inclined to think it owed its greater strength and simplicity to the fact that it was written in the first person. Immediately after this I began to 'go fancy' in a tiresome way. My one volume of autobiography records that I was trying to write well, to achieve something that could be called literature. Yes, but I was trying much too hard. I might have been saying to myself ' "Easy with the words" be damned.' I slogged my way affectedly along; it was a way of pedantry and precision, a way of whim and fuss. This way went on for seven years. I did, I suppose, evolve a style of a sort, but a rather strange sort.

In my effort to avoid hackneyed words, shopworn phrases, I was putting on handcuffs and corsets. My tight-laced prose did not, for example, allow me to use the word 'But'. Rebecca West had said in my hearing that one could usually improve the prose by taking out most of the Buts. She didn't say all. Being an all-or-nothing type, I immediately declared war on But.

In the autobiography I now read:—

'Incorrect grammar is rarely excusable.'

This statement is followed at once by: 'The use of the preposition "But" should always be avoided.' My grammatical superiority did not, alas, include the knowledge that 'But' was a conjunction.

'Always avoided' . . . yes, indeed. I could have told you

why. 'But' made, I said, a writer's comment; it exerted sentimental pressure.

Memory here restores the dining-room of a sea-side hotel where, in the year 1935, my friend John van Druten and my sister Ursula were attacking me on this point.

'Now listen,' Ursula is saying patiently, 'here's a sentence where it *must* be used: "She was feeling very ill, but she managed to grope her way out into the fresh air."'

'Why the But?' (I have said this before.)

'Because'—this is John van Druten speaking—'you're saying that although she was feeling so terrible she did get out of the room before she fell flat on her face.'

'Still there's no need for a "But" . . . I say she felt ill; I say she got out of the room. I've done my job. The "but" ought to come from the mind of the reader.'

'You know, you're crazy,' they told me. They weren't far wrong.

Another insistence was on phraseology so correct that it hurt: e.g. 'After she had opened the door and seen that which was inside.' ('What was inside'? Not on your life.) Since I developed a dislike for the look of 'Let's', all my characters had to say 'Let us', in defiance of natural-sounding dialogue. I then took a spite to the word 'it' and devised elaborate measures to avoid the use of—er—it.

Descriptions became longer and fancier. Simple movements were out. Nobody just came and went; or stood and sat. They all curved or lanced themselves, or loomed or dawned or materialised. In every phrase nuances and hints, oblique as Oriental eyes, took the place of straightforward truth. Behind this carefully-erected screen of words there was yet another screen. I had begun to be wary of letting anybody know too obviously what was going on. There is a love-scene in one novel (1934) that defies any third person's attempt to discover what these people are up to. Yet it is quite a simple occasion. The steady, faithful lover hitherto rejected, learns at last that the woman loves him. That's all. But they talk mostly about apples.

The clipping out of 'But', 'Then' and other natural links made for staccato, strutting little sentences, each in its time worked over with tremendous care, lest some vulgar, shareable manner of speech should intrude upon the pattern. Sending one of the old books to a friend in America not long ago, I wrote: 'I am afraid you'll find, as I find, that the effect of the style is like trying to read a tennis-racquet through its press.'

Even so, I observe that the autobiography, published in 1935, states solemnly: 'The presentation of a consecutive scene should be given through the eyes of only one character taking part in the scene.' Twenty-five years have gone and I still—as you know by now—agree. I was at least learning. The lesson must have done something to balance the taut, tight-rope, beware-of-the-ordinary style.

Between the years 1927 and 1939, I published about twenty books. I couldn't help travelling a certain distance. Had it not been for my straining, finicky way with the words, I should have travelled farther. Not much farther, I think, because of some handicaps that existed quite apart from my literary strivings.

I moved among my own kind. My friends were writers, actors; intelligent middlebrows who talked my own language. I knew no other world and wanted no other. My capacity for moral indignation was undeveloped. I had grown up, in two ways. In the suspect, sophisticated way that gave me a lacquer of worldliness. Far more valuably, in handing over the whole of my heart to one other person.

But my horizons were narrow still, in my thirties.

Though I had emerged from the shortest bout of atheism on record, my God was nebulous, remote: a quality upon the air, a haunt; neither to be sinned against nor served. I was content to take my standards from the man I loved. He was twenty years older than I. I sat at his feet. In the novels of 1932–39 there are portraits of him, conscious and unconscious. He was my single preoccupation. And this though it was in fact widening all horizons, seemed then to keep me happily blinkered, devoutly obsessed, even while I was working.

The last of those novels, *A Democrat Dies*, appeared, appropriately, on September 1, 1939, two days before war broke out. It vanished, with other trivia. (I am not condemning the book,—a political satire, with a crime for solving.) I don't believe I have ever met anyone who read it, outside the close circle who got their usual presentation copies. And I haven't looked at it in years. I imagine it is subject, like the rest, to that tight-laced style . . .

> *'Then the silence closed upon me*
> *till they put new clothing on me.'*

I didn't begin to write another novel until the autumn of 1946.

The expatriate who sat down with pen and paper at the kitchen table (it was the best for the purpose) in Cambridge, Massachusetts, had suffered more than a sea-change.

2

This book is no place for recording the experiences between. The years 1939–45 ripped to pieces other lives besides my own. For others, fear, agony and death became
old acquaintances, and God a friend. Enough to say that
my horizons had widened.

But it was powerfully difficult to remember how to set
about writing a novel. There were times when I cocked an
eyebrow to the memory of a talk with Storm Jameson three
years earlier. In my current disguise as Inspector of Army
Education, I had told her I thought I should find it easy
to write after the war. 'So many years,' I said 'of wanting
to do just that again, and only that.'

She didn't agree. She said that, on the contrary, it would
be much more difficult than ever before, but that I should,
on the long haul, write better books.

It was, in fact, the toughest of assignments, this new one
after the interval. The construction alone drove me half-
crazy. The characters danced rings around me. I wrote to
my father 'This is more like an illness than a novel.' I
fought all day. But I wasn't, and this was the lasting change
made by those seven years, fighting the words. The affected
strivings had ceased. The novel was by no means a great
work; but at least it was written in straight English—tem-
pered, by the demands of the background, with straight
American. Perhaps that was why, despite all the hurdles,
it took me only six months. Even so, by the time I finished
it, I had lost a stone in weight.

About twenty books in the twelve years before 1939;
only eight between the years 1946 and 1960; the pace of

production has indeed slowed down. As I said at the beginning, the tanks take longer to refill. These last eight are better books mainly because I have learned to 'be easy' with the words. (I wouldn't say however that they were being easy with me. I find my work more difficult every year.)

The choice of words is a highly individual matter. My preferences and yours cannot be the same. The feeling for certain words, or against them, is mysterious.

Why, for example, should the word 'empathy' make my hackles rise? Why should I love the words: *hazard, rope, sky, façade, fire, wave, silence, colour, shaft, courage, falcon, painted, will, air. . . ?*

Why should the word 'skill' be fine and the adding of an 's' to make the plural 'skills' give me a shudder down the back? And why should the word 'modest' arouse me to fury when used to describe something small, uncomfortable or cheap? (A modest meal; my modest means; their modest home. The adjective seems to bow from the waist in a wriggling, show-off demonstration of humility. With the implication that somebody is patting somebody else on the back for not having done better.)

The double negative is another horror. 'No mean performer'; 'not without significance'; 'by no means negligible—' . . . *Ow.*

I am, I know, curmudgeonly about abbreviations. I can no more say the word 'phone' than I can write it. Playful silliness with words, adult baby-talk such as Hoverplane for helicopter, irritates me. And the turning of nouns into verbs (e.g. a schoolboy said to have been 'truanting') drives me from the room. Another strident beast is 'airplane' for aeroplane. 'Stems from' and 'Face up to' should in my view be forbidden by law. Jargon, whether medical, technical, psychiatric, or sociological, is an enemy. The American habit of tacking 'ize' on to a noun to make a verb (hospitalize, tenderize . . .) sets my teeth on edge. Slang I incline to like, American slang particularly.

But I don't believe my taste in words to be perfect. It is just my taste.

As a congenital taker of taxis, I was continually faced some years ago by an announcement pasted on the glass panel between me and the driver. The announcement told me there would be a 'Surcharge of Sixpence on Each Hiring'. I would gladly have paid a shilling a ride to get rid of 'Each Hiring.' 'Hiring' I find eminently dislikeable and I have never been on good terms with the word 'each'. I can remember a harmless house-mistress at my first school saying 'This morning, as a special treat, there is a little piece of bacon for each one.' I desperately wanted to kill her.

Nearly thirty years ago I collaborated with Merton Hodge, the New Zealand playwright, on a movie-script. We had two serious quarrels in one day.

Merton Hodge typed: 'In the opening shot, we see an aeroplane flying over what is obviously Stockholm.'

'Flying over Stockholm,' I corrected him.

'Why?'

'All we need, isn't it?'

'*No*. We're describing this opening shot. So we have to say—'

—'No, we don't.'

'Yes, we do.'

An arbiter gave judgement in my favour. The temperature remained cool. Presently my collaborator typed: 'She enters the shop and purchases the volume.'

' "Buys the book", Merton.'

'That's what I've put.'

'No, you haven't; you've put "purchases the volume."'

'It's the same thing.'

'It couldn't be less the same thing.'

'It means exactly the same to me. I don't see the slightest difference.'

'In that case, do me a favour and make it "buys the book."'

'Why?'

He had a far better ear than mine for dialogue, and no ear for prose at all. We fought furiously again when I worked with him to turn one of his plays into a novel. He got his own back by thanking me in a foreword for my help in the 'Novelization' of the play.

The most patent help I gave him was in the descriptive passages. Merton Hodge could imitate anybody, but he could describe nothing.

The novelist can overload the descriptive passages; I myself get drunk on description easily and this tendency has to be watched. In my life many readers have told me that they abominate description. A relative of mine once went even further. 'Whenever,' said he, 'I come to a descriptive passage in one of your books, I skip it.'

'Only in one of mine?' I asked moodily. No; he was always bored with it. He just liked to be told that something was there. A lake, for example. No need to describe the lake—just say there was one. 'That,' he said sternly 'is enough for me.'

In recollection, I can see the reason for this. He had, as you might say, no eye. His bachelor-flat was a demonstration of my sister's theory that even bad taste is better than no taste at all. He wasn't interested in painting or architecture. Scenery, as he called it, bored him every bit as much as what he called Sight-Seeing bored him. He had, on the other hand, a lively interest in people and a good wave-length for human situations. Naturally he couldn't be bothered with descriptions. But I was too young to realise that this was a part of his nature. I went on at him: 'You mean—you *never* want to know how something looked?'

He said presently, 'Everything in *your* books always looks like something else.' Thus proving conclusively that he hadn't skipped all the descriptive passages: 'Here,'—he pointed out—'you say the sea looked like silver paper. Why couldn't it just look like the sea?'

The right simile, all the same, is a quarry well worth the hunt. A writer learning his trade turns naturally to this alluring search. I caught on to it first from reading Colette; and I have had much fun with it. But, oh dear, my dull relative was right when he said that everything in my early books always had to look like something else. In the attempt to shed new light, to focus on a familiar object from an unusual angle, I launched whole fleets of forced, ineffective similes. But I remember being pleased when a thrush, pulling a worm out of the ground with all his might, suggested to my mind a figure straining at the rope in a tug-o'-war. That was one of the good ones.

For the reader the right simile provokes the reaction 'Yes, of course. Why have I never noticed it before?' When Humbert Wolfe wrote:

'Like a small grey
coffee-pot
sits the squirrel'.

he gave me that flash of pleasure, that sense of discovery. Yes, of course; a squirrel sitting up did look like a coffee-pot. It still does.

(But beware the Jabberwock, my son, when your first aim as you write your description is to ensure that the tea-leaves look like ants or hyphens. It becomes a vice.)

3

Is there any short cut in the process of learning how to handle words? All I have said up till now would seem to demonstrate that there is none. Courses? Of these I know little, though I have heard much: particularly in America. When I lived in California, there seemed to be a stock question following the discovery that I was a writer and had published books: 'What courses did you take? Where did you take them?' I have studied the matter in one correspondence-course for writers. To take this course cost two hundred dollars. The first paper asked the correspondent to agree that the 'basic human emotion was insecurity' and made it clear that unless this agreement was reached, there wasn't much hope for a successful future with pen and ink.

My advice, if any young writer is listening (and it's likely that he will be far too deeply involved with his own dream) is a little different. It's mainly concerned with the length of his sentences. Heaven forbid that he should try to express himself in affected staccato as once I tried, clipping each phrase artificially. But one sign of inexperience is the long linked ramble from clause to clause. *In the manner of the nervous public-speaker who daren't pause for a moment lest he hear his own silence which would come as something of a relief to an audience already a little stunned by the barrage of words that he has been launching at them in a voice which shows only too palpably that he is under a considerable strain.* See what I mean? In the above sentence, the links are 'who', 'lest', 'already', 'in', two 'whiches' and two 'thats'. My friend the writer of the first thriller reminds me that I once scrawled acidly and face-tiously in her margin: 'Too many whiches spoil the broth'.

The first two links 'who' and 'lest' are legitimate. The clause comes to its end with the word 'silence'. What should happen here? A full-stop? Not necessarily. Punctu-ation, as I hope to show later, is an individual matter. A semi-colon might help. But the 'which' troubles me a little, in view of what's ahead. The only sound link after 'silence' is the word 'already'. An unconscious slip, you might say, of the experienced writer's pen . . . Let me see if I can do better by the whole thing:

'In the manner of a nervous public speaker who daren't pause for a moment lest he hear his own silence; silence might come, all the same, as something of a relief to an audience already a little stunned. He has been firing a con-tinuous barrage of words at them since he began; his voice is strained, unnatural.'

There, certainly, I betray my own preferences and pre-sent you with a sample of my style. But when a hitherto tractable phrase begins to snarl up and send me swinging like a monkey from clause to clause, I must see where I can stop to breathe.

That sentence is an easy one to tidy up, because it is a direct-speech, present-tense, descriptive passage; unlikely to suit the needs of fiction. Nothing easier than to give a sketch of a nervous speaker simply by talking about him. If, however, he has his place in a novel, I must treat him by the John's-eye-view method. Perhaps like this:

'From her seat in the back row, Pamela kept her eyes on the figure of Don and found that she was suffering acutely. Why was he so nervous? This wasn't, she thought, a lecture so much as a hand-gallop. It seemed he dared not pause lest he hear his own silence. Reaching the end of a phrase, he wouldn't stop; he would gabble 'Actually', 'However' and 'It seems to me,'—as he panted his way on to his next thought. Couldn't he realise that any pause, even three seconds of quiet, would come as a relief? Around her, she was aware of an audience already stunned by this barrage of words. The strained, unnatural voice might have been lunging at them for hours. Looking at her watch, she saw that he had been speaking for exactly eight minutes.'

I have, as you see, 'pulled the action nearer.' I have given you, I hope, more of a picture than you had before; this is a more urgent and visual approach. It isn't, mind you, a difficult situation to put into words.

What would be?

As far as I am concerned, the scene most vivid in my own mind is the hardest scene to make vivid on paper. I find from my notes in the volume of autobiography, that I recognised this same difficulty twenty-five years ago. Why? What, as the doctor says, seems to be the trouble?

In my head I have a colour-snapshot, the subject perfectly posed, set in sharp focus. It is more than a photograph because it is attended by subjective emotions, and likewise by palpable features recorded in memory or imagination: smells, tunes, cold, heat, damp. Let's have an example; a picture of Venice. Venice is a city I find easy to carry in my head. My eyes took their first, excited snapshots only six years ago. After that I would often start myself on the way to sleep by strolling around Venice in memory, recapturing all of it without effort. But when it came to putting a brief sketch of Venice in a novel three years later, I was much bemused. My past excitement kept jiggling the camera. I wrote broken, blurred phrases. Venice had, as it were, gone in too deep. I remember, oddly, that buying a foolscap book with a very pretty, bright-coloured cover on a sunny afternoon in Antibes, proved a help. Writing in that book, I achieved the sketch I wanted; it runs to less than a page, but it cost me hours of sweat and toil, as well as seven hundred francs for the pretty book.

Sometimes the difficulty arises from the mere fact that research has been made. When I acquire a picture deliberately rather than observe it spontaneously, the result tends to be fussy and overloaded with detail. (Excuse me, Madam, your research is showing.)

In my twenties, I made a painstaking trip to Kleine Scheidegg, to get the authentic background for a mountain adventure. I had luck. There was a moment when sunshine began to pierce a mist so thick that it had hidden even the points of my ski from my own sight. Suddenly I saw my blue shadow on the snow. The mist dazzled, thinned, until the last of it was rolling up the slopes of Eiger, Monch and Jungfrau in bright, retreating waves. (I don't think I had yet read of George Moore on the back of his donkey, gazing at the walls of Lhasa, saying to his eyes 'I beseech you to remember', but I did make a prayer of something the same kind.)

I would write of this, I told myself, as no one had ever written of mountains before. When I got back to London I remember that I lay on the floor in an all-day frenzy; scribbled sheets of paper strewn around me bore witness to my orgiastic struggling.

At this point of recollection, I have succumbed. I have taken the book from the shelf and re-read the scene. It isn't nearly as good as it ought to be; written at the peak of my affectation, its choice of words is far too grandiose. Nor can I, even now, judge it fairly as a piece of description for two reasons; one, my memory of the actual sight is still sharp; two, I found certain phrases familiar, coming to meet me in my head before my eyes found them on paper. I had them, it seems, by heart.

(Here I could wish Rebecca West hadn't said somewhere that to be familiar with his own work was the sure sign of a writer's mediocrity. It wouldn't matter to me so much if somebody else had said it, but Dame Rebecca is almost inevitably right in this kind. The only comforting contradiction I can make is that my own verbal memory, for *anybody's* words, has always been phenomenal.)

Since I published my first novel, every novelist has been able to enlarge his vocabulary. But only in one direction. In the year 1927 I sat beside my publisher's desk while he, with the required blue pencil, cut the 'Damns', the blasphemies of my youth and ignorance, the daring 'Bloody'. In my year of reading for the Book Society I found all the four-letter words in print; (so why the *Lady Chatterley* fuss?) love-making in hearty, clinical detail; blasphemies beyond my young imagining, scatological excursions; all the variations upon vice; highly elaborate descriptions of mess, smells and diseases.

Strong stuff? Mostly, I think, violence mistaken for strength. An aim for truth? More, I think, a passion for fact. (We incline to think of 'Truth' as meaning 'fact'. It doesn't. The fact of a situation is, let us say, that a wife has deserted her husband. The truth of it is that he has driven her from home by making her life unbearable.)

At least the writer of the crude word cannot be accused of trying to dodge issues. But I didn't, in my youth, always dodge the issue on purpose.

A scene that I saw with peculiar vividness and intensity before I wrote it once fooled me completely. It was concerned with lust. My character, over whose shoulder events were observed, was a strenuous, priggish fellow who had lived an ascetic life. Lust took him unawares. After staring, in an unseemly way and with the crudest thoughts, at a woman whom he was meeting for the first time, he finally picked up a prostitute on his way home. I have made it sound rather silly; but it was an honest scene, a true and necessary stage in the life of the man. I wasn't writing about sexual desire for my own fun, nor for the fun of excitable readers. Even so, when it was written, I was a little leery of it. Wasn't it too frank, too violent for its context?

When I chanced to look at it again, about two years later, I was shocked. Not, as you might imagine, by discovering that I had indeed gone too far. I hadn't gone anywhere. The exposition of lust simply wasn't there. What disturbed me in the writing of it had been thought and not said. The words were missing, the scene almost meaningless. Not as much as an overtone . . . The vivid apprehension in my own mind had deluded me and it must have been a powerful delusion to last right through the reading of galleys and page-proof.

I suspect this happens far more often than one knows. I may be easy with the words and the words may even, on occasion, be easy with me, but this is not to say that they have passed my message accurately to you.

CHAPTER
FOUR

1

'I have never,' said the Editor, speaking a little plaintively, 'seen a dash put after a comma.'

My answer might have been, but wasn't, 'Well, just stick around.'

I was at the stage where I had no views about the book under discussion; all I wanted was for it to get to the printer and stay away from my door. My deepest despair comes with my finished typescript. After these many months I am so well used to the words in my own handwriting that the handwriting itself seems an integral part of the book, now coldly lopped off by the machine. Without that protective colouring the words are always, at first blink, less right than they were.

By the time the publisher has the typescript, then, I am in no fit state to argue questions of spelling or punctuation. But this is the minute when argument arises, so argue I must. Not always effectively, nor coherently.

Spelling is constitutional. A lot of writers can't spell and a lot of people who can't write can spell. I am one of those who can spell; but I like to indulge in idiosyncrasies here and there.

There is the word 'grey'. To my mind 'grey' and 'gray' are two different shades of colour. 'Grey' has a blue tint and 'gray' a brown. So I spell the word according to the colour I want and the printer's proof-reader changes it back to uniformity throughout. Then I change it again.

There is the word 'waggon'. Sometimes I like it with one 'g'; sometimes with two. Both are given in the dictionary. The spelling of certain words must depend on their context; a matter of euphony. For example, afterwards or afterward, toward or towards, backward or backwards, forward or forwards; (can't we stop this?) Again I vary the choice. In American spelling the 's' doesn't exist, which makes things easier.

But American spelling will always be a minor trial to the English writer. I have expressed my feelings about 'airplane'. There's a clause in my American contract forbidding its use and likewise that of 'mustache'. (One of those twisted little jobs with waxed ends, if you ask me.)

The imaginary island of Leron in my unpopular novel *The Offshore Light* was governed by a Cabinet of Advisors. Repeat, Advisors. They weren't Advisers. So it's no good telling me they were. My English publishers, however, must have consulted the dictionary after I sent back the corrected page-proof. In the printed book they had all turned into Advisers and I sulked savagely for weeks.

Obviously, such eccentricities must sound a little childish, like the sulks. One mercy, for the writer who can't spell, must be the freedom from all this fuss. Or perhaps some of his misspellings are pet eccentricities too . . . I remember daring to point out to a regular correspondent of mine that 'Wensday' was not the correct way to treat the word 'Wednesday'. The reply sounded a note of outraged pain. I quote:

'*WEDNESDAY?*' Mean that's how you spell Wensday? W*ednes*day? Honestly? No kidding? It looks awful.'

From spelling to punctuation. And now for trouble. Now for the Hundred Years War. To me the punctuation is an important and oddly exciting part of the craft. It can make a power of difference, visually and aurally, to the effect I want. I must make it plain here that I find the orthodox rules for punctuation a) easy to master and b) wholly inadequate to the purposes of fiction.

Easy to master? Certainly. Look:—

'Double punctuation is not used except with quotes, parentheses, and brackets. All except ending punctuation should be dropped before a closing parenthesis . . . Neither a comma nor a dash is ever retained before a parenthetical element . . . If needed in the sentence, the comma or the dash is transferred to follow the closing parenthesis.'

Or this:

'Do not confuse a compound sentence (two or more independent clauses) with a sentence having a compound predicate (two or more verbs which have the same subject.) The comma should *not* be used between the two parts of a compound predicate.' (So sucks to you. Wait, though . . .)

'A comma *may* be used between the two parts of a compound predicate when the two verbs differ in tense or in mode (active or passive), that is when the point of view changes between two verbs.'

Well, as you see, the rules are a snip.

Why do I find them inadequate? Because they frequently fail to give the right variations in pace and emphasis. Here I'll come out on a limb and say that if you have no views on punctuation by the time you reach the age of thirty-five, you're no writer. In which case you may think that cadence cannot be affected by a comma.

But it can.

(If I wrote 'But, it can.' I should emphasise my point a little more. If I wrote 'But—it can.' I should have emphasised it still further. If I wrote 'But—it can!' I should be shouting my head off.)

Here are lines from an old book, written under the dread of war. A woman is watching and waiting for a flight of aircraft. In the second phrase, they come into view. Because the sight and the sound of them are simultaneous, I here cut out what looked like a necessary comma:

> 'That was the sound of engines, unmistakable, and those were the wings. She saw them pass roaring, in arrowhead formation, greyer than the sky.'

If I read that last sentence aloud, I cannot help coming down hard on the first syllable of the word 'roaring', and 'pass *roar*ing' with the small pause after it is the way the sight and the sound come to my eyes and ears; just a split second before the 'arrowhead formation' is observed.

The punctuation was altered in the printing of the book; the sentence read like this:

'She saw them pass, roaring in arrowhead formation, greyer than the sky.'

Obviously correct. But I couldn't settle for it, because the comma, readjusted, seemed to separate sight from sound. I changed it back.

For some inscrutable reason, the sentence stands in the book as:

'She saw them pass roaring in arrowhead formation, greyer than the sky.'

This is less good than the first, but better than the second.

A convention that makes little sense to me is the placing of the comma after the word 'said' in passages of dialogue. *David said, 'Yes.'* It seems unnecessary. What David said was 'Yes' not 'Comma, yes' nor 'Pause, yes.'

Here I can on occasion write *David said 'Yes . . .'* My use of dots and dashes has provoked many a corresponding S.O.S. from editors. If I want the end of a speech or a thought to linger, to carry over, stay on the air for a few seconds instead of blacking out quickly, I will use the dots.

By the rules, these dots, called Ellipses, do not seem to be my business at all:

> 'Ellipsis marks are used to indicate the omission from quoted matter of one or more words not essential to the immediate purpose, and also to indicate illegible words, mutilations, and similar lacunae in the original material. For English and German text, mark such ellipses by using three periods separated by 3-two-em spaces.'

Two dots, or periods, make a heresy. According to punctuation-rules, they don't exist. Sometimes they look better to my eyes than the requisite three. This was how I got a cable from America reminding me that I had used two in some places and three in others; the cable asked, thoughtfully and reasonably, whether I would grant permission for the use of three periods throughout? There was no need to cable back 'Periods habitually irregular' but I could not resist the temptation. And now I have read the proofs, I think I was wrong. Three would have looked better. But that may be only because they have spaced the two so far apart. .

My prejudices and experiments change, you see, with the years. I am just gravitating from my long love-affair with the semi-colon towards a new devotion, the colon. This may sound as meaningless as the roulette-player telling you that he has fallen out of love with the 17 and is unfaithful to it with the 29.

2

As a reader, my ear and eye for punctuation are obviously at their most strict when I'm dealing with my own manuscript. I wouldn't lay down rules for anyone else. I might occasionally question the author's choice but it is his choice and that's that.

While correcting a page-proof some years ago, I began to wonder if I were being more strict than usual. I became gloomier and gloomier. Certainly I was stale. I had only just finished with the American proofs of the same book. I was suffering from eye-skid. Was that all? Did it account for this heavy dissatisfaction, this discomfort, this feeling that something was wrong all through?

I tried to think so.

I couldn't think so.

My habit, with a page-proof, is to read it straight through, as I'd read for pleasure. When I come to a misprint or a passage that doesn't please me, I make a rapid pencil-mark in the margin and go on. I never look at the 'copy', my own typescript returned to me with the proof, until I've read the novel straight through once.

But this time I became so miserable that I went in

search of the copy before I had read halfway. Here I found the answer to my disagreeable sensations. The original punctuation had been changed all through; the editorial changes were clearly marked. This called for a re-set and a revised proof. Yet some whose judgement I respect read the first proof and found absolutely nothing wrong with the punctuation. Which may go to show that I am here a victim of the Great Fuss as opposed to the Great Relax, though I don't, of course, think so.

One of my first instructions in the whole matter was 'Never put a comma before the word "and".' This, when I was at school. Now the rules have changed. A comma before 'and' is perfectly permissible when the sense requires it. E.g.: 'He was dirty and blue with cold.' Since he wasn't dirty with cold, the comma adds to the sense. 'She loses her breath and pants' gives an image of falling underwear that can be faded out by the use of a comma. (Though I might feel that I could strengthen that elastic still more with a semi-colon; and I would, I'm sure, eventually rewrite the phrase.)

Hyphens, like cats, are capable of arousing tenderness or shudders. My father declared war on the hyphen. He joined all the words that he could join without it; and many that he couldn't. I am a hyphen-lover. You may be a hyphen hater. But there are times when you will find that its absence affects the meaning, so you have to read back:

'Her attention was caught by the blowing window curtain.'

My first fleeting impression is that the window itself is blowing. I would therefore write 'window-curtain'. But I am not consistent with my use of the hyphen and I see no reason to be. The book of rules says that hyphens are omitted 'in unwieldy combinations that could not be ambiguous.' (The image here, to somebody my age who recalls wearing 'combinations' is beguiling, but that's by the way.) The two examples given are:

(i) encyclopedia compiler.
(ii) materials gatherer.

This illustrates my theory that the rules are inadequate for fiction:

'With a cry of joy she fell into the arms of the encyclopedia compiler.'
'Drawing his flick-knife he stabbed furiously at the materials gatherer.'

My first fleeting impressions are highly ambiguous. How are yours? Surely hyphens would help?

(Mind you, I know what the rules mean: they mean one's eyes cannot possibly be as silly as that: one will scarcely need to pause to discover that she didn't fall into the encyclopedia's arms; that the assailant wasn't stabbing at the materials. But fiction, I have stipulated, keeps me, the reader, wholly involved and engaged. I am not on the look out for 'unambiguous' qualities; I'm living with, and in, the novel.)

Besides being a hyphen-lover I am a bracket-lover. The snare (here) is that I (quite often) find almost any clause (no matter what its context) worthy of a bracket. See?

I have been the cause of irritation to editors and readers alike with my trick of setting brackets around the quotes in a panel of dialogue, to indicate a thought that goes unspoken:

'Are you happy, Jim?'
('And if I wasn't, I couldn't tell you. How could I?')
Or even in a panel of prose:

The room was dim, with the greyness of early morning.
('I hate this room; I always have.') There was a still, dusty
haunt here; a smell of age and damp.

I try to guard against over-indulgence with the brackets.
But I find them immensely useful. (If I didn't, they could
go jump in the lake.)

When I set down the characters' thoughts, my decision
whether to enclose them in quotes or leave them plain may
seem wholly arbitrary. It isn't:

> *An action entirely typical of her, he thought: she
> would do this and nothing else.*

The last thing I want here is a cluster of quotes. The
thought is expressed a little more heavily than it would
be if he were merely thinking aloud. He is down at a deeper
level, going at a slower pace. His thought doesn't take the
form of direct, spontaneous speech. Set in quotes, it as-
sumes a slight pomposity:

'An action entirely typical of her,' he thought. 'She
would do this and nothing else.'

Were he thinking rapidly, colloquially, from the top of
his mind, I should use quotes; but not those words. I should
probably write: "'How exactly like Mabel,' thought Arthur."

There is a context in which I find the word 'said' more
effective than the word 'thought', though I do not mean
that the character spoke aloud. 'Said to himself' would be
clumsy:

If only, he said, he could get her out of his mind once and for all.

There is a nuance here. The phrase shows, or should at least hint, that the thought has been thought before; that the character is nagged by it. That's what I had in view. The editor amended it to read 'If only,' he said, 'he could get her out of his mind . . .' thereby driving me out of mine.

You may have noticed that when Arthur thought 'How exactly like Mabel', he didn't use an exclamation-mark. This is, I know, an arbitrary omission. One result of my long war with the exclamation-mark in prose is to deny it automatically to my characters in dialogue. I can give no convincing reason for my horror of '!' The only place I like it is upside down at the beginning of the phrase, as in Spanish, where it looks quite decorative.

A book of mine was republished in a paper-back edition. When I got the proof I saw, to my sorrow, that somebody had gone all through it, scattering exclamation-marks where he would. It took me four days to remove these dragon's teeth and the publisher's acknowledgement pleased me little: 'I note,' he said 'that you do not like exclamation-marks. I hope, however, that you are not going to put us to the expense of taking them all out.' I was. I did. During the battle he assured me that their use was correct and I assured him that I would sue him if a single one appeared. He has never, I think, felt the same about me since.

'A hideous fuss about nothing,' said the friend to whom I told the story. But the friend wasn't a writer. The next writer I saw was Duff Cooper, at Chantilly the following week-end. 'Would you,' I asked him 'have left them in or taken them out?' The effect was explosive. We were at dinner. Duff Cooper put down his knife and fork. His last book had just appeared in the same paper-back edition; he had not opened it; he must go and open it now. Diana Cooper suggested that, since legal proceedings could not be instigated from Chantilly to London on a Saturday night, he might as well finish his dinner. A thunderous interval followed. He was robbed of his grievance by finding no exclamation-marks. He was consoled because I hated them too. Comrades in phobia, we drank the midnight out.

3

Among the functions of the copy-editor in America, I once read, was to 'ensure a better-looking page, with uniformity of punctuation, paragraphing, etc.' by the process of 'styling' the manuscript. I re-read the manifesto; the 'etc.' seemed particularly ominous. 'But paragraphs?' I said to myself. 'Now there's a mysterious thing. Surely the division of paragraphs must be the writer's affair and nobody else's.'

The end of a paragraph, the switch to a new line, affects speed and cadence.

> *Suddenly he knew he could stand no more of it. 'Please go,' he said. She went.*

> *Suddenly he knew he could stand no more of it. 'Please go,' he said.*
> *She went.*

Suddenly he knew he could stand no more of it.
'Please go' he said.
She went.

All three have different speeds, therefore different effects. As a writer I like to experiment with the effects; which is one reason why I mourn the lost days of the galley-proof. Galleys still come from America, but not, it appears, from London publishing houses. A page-proof, all set, gives one no chance to play around.

But, wistfully, I must admit that once the novel is in proof the fun is over anyway. It used not to be so. If I sound peevish about publishing methods, it is partly because I have long lost the first fine careless rapture of seeing my work in print, and partly because the whole publishing scene has changed completely in the last thirty years. I look back now on a process that moved at a gentle, friendly jog-trot; where there was no editor nor copy-editor; where every stage was pleasurable and exciting; where we took days discussing the design for the book-jacket and mine was the only novel of any importance to the firm. Well, if that wasn't true, (and it wasn't) that was how it felt.

Is it an illusion that I used not only to write before breakfast, but read proofs or typescript in an excited ferment before breakfast? One of my abiding instructions to myself now (no matter what stage the book has reached) is *Don't think about it before breakfast.*

And not too soon after breakfast, either. One cigarette, or two cigarettes, first. Why? Because the early-morning mood for me is a killer of the dream, a spoiler of the fun. It is flat, detached, unkind. It can inform me, if I let it, that my current work is worthless, and then proceed to hold up a cool, jeering mirror to all I have written. All that seemed so fine last night is wrong and silly. '*Remember this phrase? That phrase? Well, did you ever hear such stuff?*' He lies, the morning monster.

But there are nights when I leave my work feeling truly discouraged and go to bed in a gloom. These doubts are genuine. And then I deliberately invite the monster to breakfast next morning. In his abominable, let-me-off-nothing way, he can help me to sort the trouble out.

4

Could any outside opinion do that? Am I living—more and more—in an Enclosed Order of my own?

This reflection is in part aroused by looking again at G. B. Stern's *One Is Only Human*, a book that has many good things in it.

The question before the house is this:—

> 'Would you still have an unconquerable compulsion to write a book if marooned on a desert island without hope of rescue?'

In the discussion there are two points of view. One: that the writer wouldn't be able to help conceiving a book, but might shun the physical drudgery of writing it, since it would never be read. Two: that the creative power within would not be satisfied until the book was actually written —reader or no reader.

Heckling myself, I find out these things. I should write the book because I couldn't help writing it,—given the foolscap and the pens. Moreover, there is nothing I would want to do so much. On the island, the book would, I believe, pursue its inevitable course: the three processes, the beckoning Idea, the laborious Rough, the speedier Smooth. I should be happy; I should be gloomy; I should soar into exaltation and plunge heavily down. Just as I do now. Provided that the foolscap was illimitable and the ink didn't run out, I might live my second life more vividly and successfully on a desert-island than I do in Hampstead. Why?

More leisure? No. Every book dictates its own deadline, preserves its own tempo, makes its own demand to be finished. I cannot imagine this particular drive halted by my knowledge that I had all the time in the world (or out of it . .) before me. The same devils of idleness would beckon me there as here. And the same doubts; the same lack of confidence at the start. But these would, by virtue of the spell, be vanquished: as they are here.

There would be no shopping to do; no laundry to be counted; no telephone. My cooking, I think, would be a simple and time-saving affair, once I'd got the hang of the cocoanuts; once I had discovered, without dying, which were the edible fish and vegetables.

Loneliness would be the worst of it. In my loneliness I should need and acquire company, the company of my trade; the characters, the invaders of solitude, walking in.

I imagine I would spend longer hours than I spend now on revisions, the second and third thoughts that come between the Rough and the Smooth. And I should, as soon as my various physical handicaps allowed, have a happily indulgent session, doing a second Smooth: a final draft, a perfect draft wherein the handwriting was as good as could be, all the ugly crossings-out eliminated, the margins neat and straight.

For whom? No typist in need of such deferential treatment. No publisher. And no reader. Somehow, shockingly perhaps, this last thought worries me not at all. I would, I know, be sad about it when the work was done. What I see now is that life on a desert-island without writing a novel would be unbearable; to write would make it bearable. If this was a fate enforced then I could be resigned, at peace and having a tolerable time, given pens and paper.

Which provokes me to ask what sort of animal is the novelist who feels as I do? Not, I know, an unusual animal . . . But what makes and sustains him? Is there one single quality possessed by him at the start that preserves him always, devotedly slaving?

I think it is simply the power of his imagination.

CHAPTER

FIVE

1

'With a host of furious fancies
whereof I am commander . . .'

In a child, the gift of imagination is suspect, something
of a sin. ('It's all your imagination': 'You're just making
it up.') Even 'That child has such an imagination' sounds
a faintly uneasy note.

In the adult, the virtue of imagination has this in common with the virtue of courage. Without it, you are less
good: with it, you are not necessarily better. Though a
mort of human sins and troubles come solely from a lack
of imagination, its possession may likewise engage you in
unprofitable exercises:—Lying; slandering; over-anxiety;
over-embroidery; painting devils on walls, other people's
walls as well as your own.

The first important lie I ever told won me a bronze medal.
I was eight years old and it was, as you might say, a writer's
lie: a Nature Note for the magazine called *Little Folks*.

I had seen, I wrote, a mother-rabbit in flight from the
corncutters, carrying a baby rabbit in her mouth while
two more baby rabbits ran beside her. I had seen nothing

of the kind. I was, I suppose, bored with the run-of-the-mill nature notes which I contributed regularly: records of catkins, birds'-nests and such. Though as a rule a prey to tormenting guilt, I felt no sense of sin when the medal came. I was just surprised and pleased. I wore it by day and kept it in its box at night.

I lied as much as children commonly lie and for the common reason—to keep out of trouble. But I lied also when there was no need except my own passionate need for drama. Reporting a minor illness to my mother from school I wrote that the housemistress had 'looked serious', when she had laughed merrily, telling me there was no need for alarm. Having scraped my knuckle, I deliberately jabbed the scrape with a penknife to make it look worse before exhibiting it. I invented sinister remarks overheard; 'a long low whistle' coming from the trees at night; a string of fantasies concerned with my own childhood—all greedily believed by my school friends. I thirsted for drama all the time. If it wasn't available I made it up.

I have a theory that all children are novelists and dramatists inside. I remember the small classroom with the Rectory children, at Honiton, when I was happy and believed we would always live there. I used to half-shut my eyes, blur the look of the room with my lashes, and think, in delicious melancholy: 'This is how it will look when it is all long, long ago and I am remembering it.'

The time to be going, the time for boarding-school, the end of Devonshire, came in 1918. For days before we left, I used to halt in front of the large looking-glass in the bathroom, flinging back my head, clasping my temples, posed as dramatically as I could. To myself I was repeating *'The death of a whole past life, the birth of a whole new'*—from Charles Kingsley's *Westward Ho!*

The sentence, which concerns the Indian girl, Ayaca-nora, continues thus: *'were struggling in those magnificent eyes, choking in that magnificent throat.'* I regret to say I finished the sentence every time. (But I have probably misquoted, because I haven't read the book since.) When the day of departure came, there was no drama at all; only plain misery: then long, long hours in a wartime train, singing tunelessly (I had just been reading *Red Pottage*) *Wrap me up in my old stable-jacket*. It seemed an appropriate dirge.

True drama in childhood had the effect of silencing me completely. Making illusory magic was so much a part of my routine that when magic really walked in I was stunned by awe and excitement. And it became a secret, not to be told.

At school, at the age of eleven, I was playing a game of explorers up the Amazon; crawling along the course of a narrow dried-up ditch in a little wood. I was the leader of the expedition; the expedition was a child named Joyce Boake.

Most of these games I still played in the third person: a ruling devised by my sister and myself at Honiton. When we spoke our parts we would add 'said Hercules' or 'said Buffalo Bill' and describe the action as though we were writing a story aloud. So, on this occasion, the leader (whose name has vanished) 'gave a warning shout. "A snake!" he cried. "A monster! Be still. It may not attack us . . ."'

I had, in fact, sighted a thick coil of dusty rope in the ditch about a yard ahead. Obedient to the game, the expedition stayed as still as I. The rope promptly uncoiled and slithered away into the scrub: the biggest grass-snake I have ever seen. In memory it still looks like a python.

Nothing would induce me to tell Joyce that I had made up the snake from a likely-looking piece of rope. She mustn't know I felt like Merlin . . . or Aaron.

I was only ten when I saw my first ghost, at the school called 'Claremont' in Eastbourne. It happened in broad daylight. It couldn't, I knew, be anything but a ghost; it was very frightening and it disobeyed one of the Queensberry rules for phantoms by reflecting itself in a looking-glass.

The glass was on the door of a cupboard. The cupboard stood on the landing at the top of the stairs. As I came up the stairs, the cupboard door stood ajar and the door of my bedroom was wide open. The angled glass reflected a part of the room. I looked at the reflection: it showed somebody coming across the bedroom floor.

I had time to be puzzled. I shared the room with my sister and one other child; surely I had just left them both in the garden? I had time to think 'Who's this?' before it ran out of the bedroom door to meet me: a humped, white shape, like a dwarf. It scuttled straight to the middle of the landing and then it wasn't there.

No light-effect, no shadow, could account for it. It was a solid thing, seen first in the glass, then coming between me and the glass. There was no need to urge myself not to tell. I knew I wouldn't tell. Nor did I, until after I was grown-up.

A rope that conjured itself into a grass snake four feet long? A daylight ghost with a reflection? Did I realise that whereas the first story was too good to be true, the second was by no means good enough? Perhaps. For a talkative child, I kept odd silences. My terrors stayed untold. There was the terror of sex. The sexual act was first described to me, all wrong and on a note of religious pomposity, by a girl of twelve called Margaret Reuss. I can see her face, and the garden behind her. When she had finished telling me I said automatically 'I'm sure my father and mother didn't do anything like that.' Afterwards, my imagination played with the thought for a while. She had left out the necessity for a bed altogether. Her preliminary: 'Some time after you are married, your husband comes to you and asks you if you want a child' suggested a highly formal occasion. I saw them doing whatever it was they were supposed to do (she had mentioned 'the lower quarters of the body') standing up, in a drawing-room, with some special kind of table between them, so that the proprieties were observed. This picture didn't frighten me; it just seemed mysteriously silly. The terror only began at the age of fourteen after I knew that the sexual act was an informal procedure in bed and 'sleeping together' meant just that. Why it should have been alarming I can't imagine. I talked in a pretence of sophistication: I was allowed to read books and see plays whose theme included adultery. I was assumed, by my teachers and my chums, to 'know'. All I knew was the dotted line, the gap in the words, before the chapter ended and by the next chapter it was usually the next morning.

My imagination stopped dead at the dotted line. It had to; I was too scared to let it go further. I remember my mother giving me permission to read a current novel, adding that the last chapters dealt with infidelity and divorce; if any of that worried me, I was to tell her. Certainly it shouldn't have worried me. I was fifteen; I was already a child of divorce, and my mother was somebody from whom I would have told you I had no secrets. The thing I didn't tell her was that I dared not read those chapters; I merely pretended I had.

I can remember—at the same age—having jitters all day because we were going to see a movie called *Foolish Wives*, starring Erich von Stroheim. It was luridly advertised as a Sex-Picture. I had no claims to piety. I seldom prayed except at night, but on that day I knelt down solemnly by my bed in the afternoon and prayed for the film not to be too frightening. It turned out to be an innocuous matter. Herr von Stroheim was seen in a cloud of creeper at the bedroom-window (to an accompaniment of ominous chords on the piano) while the lady, whose name escapes me, slept, unaware of the approaching rape. They cut from there. My relief was enormous and I duly said 'Thank you' in my night prayers.

It occurs to me, irrelevantly, that I wrote the end of my first novel on that day, after we came home from the movie. Its title was *The Primrose Way* and it concerned a lady tennis-champion. Her name was Sally and she had a habit of wearing a 'rose-coloured teagown' when off the court. There was no sex in the story. Though happily married, the lady couldn't have children, nor did I ever imagine her in bed with her splendid fair-haired husband. She died, of course. She skidded her car so as not to run over a dog. Nobody knew. Her husband 'murmured "Yes, darling" uncomprehendingly' when, on her deathbed, she prompted him to reassure her that the sacrifice had been worthwhile. I bade her farewell, in a bath of tears, with the words 'So the road runs, Sally . . . into the sunset.'

Death didn't frighten me at all in those days. I was forever picturing my own death, playing a whole variety of deathbed scenes in enthusiastic detail. And where ghosts were concerned (apart from the one real apparition) I thoroughly enjoyed scaring myself. I read every ghost story I could find and told them aloud at school, after lights-out, until somebody had a nightmare and the practice was banned.

I am still fascinated by ghosts, and have met many. My profession doesn't send me ghost-hunting every day. But on reflection I think the novelist must be always something of a ghost-hunter. The mind of every human being is haunted ground and the writer's imagination leads him on; not as a Member of the Psychical Research Society, explicitly studying phenomena; he is drawn into the human mysteries without being consciously aware of the process. He doesn't have to act Hawk-Eye the Detective, either. His explorations are the automatic work of his type of mind.

The word 'compassion' is so greatly overworked in the assessment of creative literature today that I wish there was another word. But the quality is, or should be, one immediate product of the novelist's imagination. Should he come to maturity and still be without compassion, he will be the lesser artist for that.

The first time I was aware of it—not just of 'being sorry' for somebody, but of being involved with the person, linked with her in a way that I could not understand—I have never told and never written. At the time it hurt too much and I packed it away.

I was seventeen. I had come up to London for the day from Windsor. London, before I got a job there, was Tom Tiddler's Ground, with the promise of adventure just around the corner. The time was early morning. Just why I was wandering through the writing-room in Selfridge's I don't know; but the room was almost empty: only one person sitting at a small table, busy with pen and ink. I passed close to her. She was writing a letter painstakingly, in a large clear hand. Two other letters, already written, stamped and addressed, were propped up in front of her. She was a middle-aged woman. Before I saw the writing on the paper, I had noticed that she was ugly: not grotesque, merely ugly; with a tight mouth, a blob of a nose. She wore steel-rimmed spectacles. Her hair, flat and colourless, was strained back from a big shiny forehead.

On the paper these words were written: 'I should tell you I am not young nor at all of good appearance.'

Well, I haven't, as I said, tried writing that small episode down before. I find that the passage of thirty-five years has made remarkably little difference to my feelings about it. I remember going through the London day, that should have glittered, vainly trying to pretend it hadn't happened. But it had; it was inside me, lodged in me. It wasn't only pity. There was no sense of separation from her; she didn't trouble me from a depth. I wasn't on a height. I was somehow that woman, and she was myself. We were mixed up together, hurt together; miserable together. I kept wishing I had stopped and said something nice, and then reminding myself grimly that there was nothing 'nice' to say.

That was the first time. I have often had the feeling since: it doesn't necessarily come with pity. I have 'been' Denis Compton scoring his century, Maria Bueno throwing her racquet in the air when she won the match, a child climbing the railings at the Zoo to watch the sea-lions, a woman selling flowers in South Carolina.

Geoffrey Winthrop Young, in his mountains, called the feeling that of 'being a bead on a string.'

I was aware of it one night in '44, when the buzz-bombs were coming over. We stepped off the tube-train on to the platform at Green Park Station. The platform was crowded, right up to the edge, with the people who had come down there to sleep. We had to walk carefully so as not to step on them: mothers, children, babies; old men, old women; closely-packed bodies lying still. My two A.T.S. companions who had no fear of the bombs, laughed at the sleepers as we picked our way. But I was afraid and I was them all, and I couldn't laugh.

2

In the course of writing novels, there is one hurdle my imagination will never take. That is the task of describing a place I haven't visited. I have invented islands, towns, villages, landscapes, gardens. But if the place is to be found on the map I can't draw an imaginary picture of it. I have to go there and see. No photographs, no descriptions rich in detail, no amount of guide-book reading can loosen the shackles of my intimidation, to let me wander there freely in my head. I do not know what makes this failure. Only twice have I been obliged to go on in spite of it.

The first time, I was twenty-two. A plan to sail to South Africa had inspired the dream of a novel whose whole action was set on the liner. When the journey was cancelled, I still wanted to write the novel—and did, though my longest sea-voyage to date was Folkestone-Boulogne. I only dared it because the story was largely an indoor affair, beds, bar-life, card-rooms. When it was done, I had it checked by somebody who had made the voyage. There seemed to be few mistakes. But any experienced traveller who read that book must, I am sure, have guessed the truth.

The second time couldn't be avoided because I needed the hundred pounds too badly. The commission was a short Biblical biography, one of a series. My allotted subject was

Jezebel. ('We agreed, the publisher and I', said my agent, 'that you were just the person for Jezebel.')

I spent long, unhappy days at the London Library. Most of the authorities, I found, were in German. I emerged with a tenderfoot's instruction in Baal-worship and some rather pretty stuff about fishing for the murex off the Phoenician coast. A talk with Dr. Cecil Roth completed my researches. My only other equipment consisted of a map and a Bible.

Like all alarming encounters, this one had to be tackled quickly, before I lost my nerve. I wrote it in three weeks. Once I had settled for my own method, I enjoyed the assignment. The only thing to do was to work my way into the characters' heads: nobody could challenge the liberties I took there. As I wrote, the three great figures, Jezebel, Ahab and the prophet Elijah, became true for me; I believe I took one of my slow, retarded steps nearer to God while I was writing of Elijah.

When my courage finally failed, it failed for good reason. Though I had not feared to paraphrase and expand many scenes from the Bible story, I cowered before the majesty in the last verses of all. Nobody I thought, could tamper with those. So I faded out my book before they came:

> *Now, if she put out her foot for one more step, she would stand by the window. Were they whispering behind her? Those were arrows that whispered, flighting from the roof-top. That was the tide, breaking on the palace wall.*
> *'It would be foolish to wait,' she said.*
> *She took one more step.*

On the last page, the recto page, facing this one, I quoted the six verses that begin: '*And as Jehu entered in at the gate, she said "Had Zimri peace, who slew his master?"*'

They made my own words look small, but it was the best I could do.

(Perhaps because I was never audacious enough to try anything of the sort again, I still have an affection for the Jezebel biography. The series came to nothing: I think only one writer besides myself finished the job; I remember only one review.)

3

There is another kind of failure in my imagination; a perfect pig. When it afflicts me I know I must look out. If I don't look out, here comes falseness at a run.

The moment is usually signalled by the feeling: 'Oh, I *can't* . . .' and the obstacle is always a peak situation, a scene of importance in the book. Since I'm not entirely aware of my own mysteries, I don't necessarily diagnose my own failure to follow through. All I know is that I want to duck this large issue. It must, I tell myself, be obliquely approached, glossed-over, told at secondhand by one of the characters: somehow I must soft-pedal it by presenting it indirectly. Because I just can't write it straight, the way I'd planned.

Why not? I have to know. Surely if there was a subtle, effective way of showing the big truth, the big moment, I wouldn't be saying 'Oh I *can't*'; I'd be saying 'Hullo: I can do it better like this.' So I heckle myself patiently and presently discover that I'm just plain frightened of it.

It might be a murder scene. It might be a scene of huge,

heroic self-sacrifice. It might be a piece of damnable behaviour, like robbing an old-age pensioner. It might be a homosexual love scene. It could be anything.

Once I know it frightens me, I can be done with my attempts at rationalisation. I have suggested to myself variously that the situation is unreal, that it won't 'work', that it isn't really important, that the characters concerned won't play it after all. But the examination of my literary conscience has disproved every one of these excuses.

I must go down deeper:

(1) *'I never robbed an old-age pensioner: I couldn't: I don't know how it feels. It's too revolting.'*

'You have, in your time, stolen a piece of toffee; cheated the Customs; conveniently forgotten a debt; pocketed the money you found on a taxi-floor; helped to destroy a reputation; denied a vulnerable person a kindness and seen the look in that person's eyes.'

(2) *'I have never performed an act of heroic self-sacrifice, handing over the man I loved to somebody else. I couldn't.'*

'You have given one of your favourite possessions to a friend who wanted it—and you miss it still. You have let somebody else go to the play because there was only one ticket. You have said "No" to a really beguiling invitation because you wouldn't break a dull date with a dull person who was in great trouble. You've refused good money for writing something that your conscience couldn't approve.'

(3) *'I've never picked up a knife and stabbed a boy in the neck.'*

'You've been drunk; you've lost your temper; you have hated. You have slapped somebody's face—hard.'

(4) *'I am not a homosexual male of twenty-five.'*

'You know what love is, how it feels to be in love, to make love. Your literary technique and your literary manners should be good enough by now to stop this winsome backing-away. Get on. And remember that you are not out to describe a clinical clinch, but the reality of an emotion.'

By the time I am engaged on this kind of exercise, I'm well on the way to writing the scene. I am also making a voyage of discovery that reveals once again the presence of the rabbit inside. The voyage has been going on for years. The proper exercise of my imagination demands, I believe, that no human situation should ever be too large, too painful, too frightening, too shocking, for me to face. Anything that I can face, in my own truth, I can write.

Does this last observation sound self-satisfied? It shouldn't. My reach has been exceeding my grasp for more than thirty years. I don't mean when I say 'I can write it' that I can give it the Dickens treatment, the Tolstoy treatment or the Kipling treatment. And while I ponder that, I believe I should have harnessed the quality of discontent with imagination when I began the chapter. This surely is the other necessity for the novelist.

Given the ready ear, the open eye, the desire and the stamina, he will travel: but slowly. Technique is the tool of his trade to be acquired only by years of hard work. No creative writing-course can give him that. There is no knowledge of it to be taken in tabloid form. It is the acquisition that comes to him gradually; by way of writing much that will please him as he writes, only to fall short of his demands in a year's time. To be unsatisfied with his achievement in spite of praise is at the heart of him. I believe that in the difference between a writer and a hack, the discontent is all.

4

And where is it taking him? What is his aim when he sets out? (I can remember mine at the beginning: to be a poet. But not all the furious fancies whereof I was commander could do that; I have no music in me.) What is his aim, as he goes on, the target his discontent will never let him reach? Is there a target at all, other than the work for the love of the work itself? In an attempt to define it, I would say that his target is to tell his own truth in the best possible words. Truth again . . . The paradox remains; the novelist can write truth when he writes fiction; and the safest way to preserve that truth is to get it between covers.

No magazine nor newspaper can be a wholly reliable medium. Not because either is, necessarily, a seller of falsehood, but because both are hampered by considerations irrelevant to the writer:—space, policy, advertisers, topical angles. The same shackles may apply in more or less degree to film-work, to T.V. and broadcast-scripts.

To which there is an obvious retort: 'I want to reach the widest possible audience. I have a great deal to say. Surely it's no sort of dishonesty to use the mass-media whenever I can? To keep an eye to topical angles? I want to be a writer of my own times, not a mediaeval monkish solitary, with the study door forever shut, and the curtains drawn. You make me feel I'm threatened with corruption from the moment I put pen to paper.'

I have news for you; you are.

CHAPTER

SIX

1

At nineteen I saw no problem in writing as I wanted to write and earning good money by doing just that. I had arrived most innocently on the scene of success.

Three novels followed the epic of the lady lawn-tennis champion. One I abandoned within sight of the end; partly because it was about killing my father and partly because I had to take School Certificate. The other two were finished and rejected. (I remember that I tried each of these on one publisher only: I carried the parcel to the august office myself: in due course I read the unfavourable report that came back and then put the typescript away.)

The fourth novel was accepted. The sales were big. I looked ahead to a life wherein I could always write as I pleased and always earn these delicious sums of money. The money was so much a part of the fun, so happily taken for granted, that I couldn't in those days have told you the difference between commerce and art.

I had this in common with other innocents: my integrity was simply me. We didn't part company for several years. All writing was worthwhile. I had no doubts, no dilemma. Any commission was an amiable challenge, to be accepted at once. A short story wanted by a magazine meant that I wanted to write a short story. I was bubbling with ideas anyway and the price was merely an extra inducement to get one or another idea down on paper. It was a lot of fun. I thought it would go on forever.

When the gold splurge of 1927–29 came to its ashy ending, I was left with two loads: unrequited love and unpaid debts. The first made writing difficult: the second made it imperative.

In an effort to cope with the situation I put aside a half-finished novel and accepted a commission from the *Daily Mirror* to write a serial. The stipulations were sixty thousand words, love, and a happy ending. I would, I thought grimly, write my own story—with a difference. The heroine must discover in the last instalment that she loved the more suitable of the two gentlemen after all. And I should have three hundred pounds to pay off the debts.

Never before had I worked to so rigid a time-table. Never before had work been so joyless: a chore, a daily stint, hammered out in two winter months that seemed very long indeed. I met the deadline. The serial was turned down. I remember feeling a kind of justice in this, though it was hideously disappointing. I had written for money alone and the money had eluded me.

'Much too sophisticated for our readers' the editor said. So—for the first time—I became conscious of the customers and the need to please them if I wanted the cash.

My publisher offered to read the serial, with a view to producing it in book form. But I couldn't agree: I was too much ashamed of it. So the debts hung around while I finished the novel and I don't believe I was solvent again for ten years. In all that time I wrote as regularly as I could for newspapers and magazines, with an eye to the market.

My perspective had changed. Writing what I wanted to write and writing for money had become two different things.

Still I protected the novels, seeing them as a wholly different cast of work from the journalism and the magazine-stuff. Only once, ever, did I write a novel for the sake of the advance. It was a plague to me; I knew how bad it was; it nearly got itself thrown into the Mediterranean half-way along. And when I had bludgeoned myself on to finish it . . . ? I feel somebody would be pleased to hear how good it was, how well it was reviewed, how splendidly it sold. No; it was as poorly received as it deserved to be. (I recall a letter from Rebecca West beginning 'You should have your bottom heavily spanked for this book', which was about the kindest observation in the whole letter and, like the rest of it, quite fair.)

The amount of hack-work I did 'on the side' from 1929 till 1939 was considerable. Meanwhile, my integrity and I conducted regular bouts of shadow-boxing. Why? What was wrong in writing for the newspapers? In my articles on love-and-all-that for the women's magazines?

Let me begin with the magazines. I seldom write for them now. When I do I am not at ease. They still incline to want love-and-all-that. I have, in my time, enjoyed working for them and they have grown up more than a little in thirty years. Yet, as others have said, there remains something cosily false in their approach. No matter what they're approaching. In Magazine-Think, it's deliciously easy to make a dress from a paper pattern or whip up a soufflé, provided you follow the directions. (This is not true.) On the other hand it is excessively difficult to keep the affection of the man you love, even after he has married you. This isn't true, either. But according to Magazine-Think, it *can* be done, provided you follow the directions: it isn't impossible: a matter of eye-shadow, psychology, personal fragrance and other deft little feminine touches. It's a life-work, a thing to slog away at; unlike the simple and speedy tasks of cooking, housekeeping, dressmaking, dish-washing, child-bearing and interior decoration.

All good clean fun, the women's magazines and entirely innocuous. My attitude to the popular press was, and is, quite different. This may best be illustrated by the fact that I wrote under contract to a woman's magazine for five years and was never once tempted to break the agreement: whereas, after only three years' work for a daily paper, I flung the contract in the editor's face. I don't mean I threw a physical document in his face. But he looked as though I had. It was a good offer and he knew I needed the money.

'I'm sorry,' I said. 'I just don't want to do it any more.'

'Why not?'

I couldn't explain why not.

'What are you going to live on?'

I said I had no idea.

We weren't quarrelling; we liked each other; we had known each other a long time.

'But this is a year's contract we're offering you,' he said patiently. 'Same terms as before.'

When I still refused it, he told me I was obstinate and unreasonable. 'Just like your father' he added: he loved my father, so I took it as a compliment. The conversation stopped there because Lord —— called him, and in common with all Lord ——'s editors he went down on his knees to answer the telephone.

I walked out of the office feeling light and happy. Looking back twenty years to the self who did the silly thing, I know she was right.

There's no harm in writing for newspapers if that's the way you're made. I wasn't made that way. I made myself that way for a time and for the wrong reasons. Why do I believe that I must 'keep my distance and my soul' from the popular press?

First and most obviously, the standard of the work required is necessarily lower than the standard to be met in writing a novel. Not merely different, but lower. The end in view is for the customers to buy the paper. You may be very good at making the customers buy the paper if you can write the kind of column they care for. But unless you are a specialist,—like a sports-writer or a fashion-writer or a cookery-expert,—your first task is to turn out a 'good story'; which, briefly, means distorting the truth. You must, as a journalist, perform circus-tricks. Eye-catching phrases, over-statements, neat omissions and heavy slants will become your business. If you are successful in these devices, then your success will probably seem a more important affair than it is. Because you are moving in a world where publicity is a thing-in-itself; a world of names; a world full of favourites and idols and *impresarios de rien*. A band-wagon world.

The first time I ever recognised the band-wagon was at the age of thirteen. Naturally I didn't give it that name, nor any name. On Sunday evenings we were, by the rules of the house, allowed to eat our sweets. It was the custom to bring out the boxes sent by our parents and offer them round: the air was loud with: 'Have one of mine?' 'Thanks awfully; have one of mine?'—'Thanks awfully.' The supplies varied, of course. Some of my companions, I noticed, never ran out of sweets; their mothers kept them stocked from the beginning of term to the end. Huge boxes of chocolates, fat tins of toffee, slabs of coconut ice went on and on appearing, Sunday after Sunday.

For some, like myself, there was a regular hiatus, a week or more when we had nothing to offer. Soon I discovered that when you had no sweets, nobody gave you any. I remember an evening when my share of the treasure amounted to one boiled sweet, prised from a sticky, almost-empty bag. The girl who offered it was a dumb, dumpy, unpopular creature; I, with the rest, had teased her and made a butt of her. I don't know if I felt guilty about that: I hope I did. From my corner, pretending to read, I watched the Olympians handing their great boxes to one another; the glad cry of 'Thanks awfully' rang in my ears and the crunching, sucking noises went on.

Next Sunday was different. Two splendid parcels from Fuller's had come for me during the week and I brandished them before the Olympians who in their turn gambolled about me saying 'Have one of mine,' while I said 'Thanks awfully.' I had the sense of luxurious achievement, of being on the favoured side: a feeling that I have known since, at roulette, when the numbers are coming up. I enjoyed it very much. But I wasn't deceived. Without cynicism, without rancour, I made an automatic note in my head. I can't recall the words of it; maybe there were no words. I just knew I had learned something. (And for all my truck with the Olympians, I did give first choice from both boxes to the girl whose sticky boiled sweets had now run out.)

This experience may seem perhaps to rate among Blinding Glimpses of the Obvious. But I had heard the cliché 'Nothing succeeds like success' many times before I saw what it meant. It meant Sunday evening and the sweets.

This lesson has lasted. I have never seen the simple fact disproved. There are friends—and there are band-waggoners; and one may blush for the band-waggoners but that's about all one can do. They are caught in the rat-race after the bitch-goddess, even if they do not compete personally. For them, limelight reflects, and they must be near enough to the source for the reflection to touch them. According to J. B. Priestley the band-wagon and the rat-race are almost exclusively male preoccupations. Only the worst bitches among women, he says, pursue the bitch-goddess. (If that's true, some of my best friends are bitches, said my best friend . . .)

Anyway, the popular press has this matter deep at its heart and must therefore be shunned by me. But the band-wagon makes a fascinating study. There are certain pilot-fish to be observed as the rout goes by; the anti-success boys who only want to see the well-paid, well-loved idol knocked off his pedestal: the snipers and the snide-mongers. Sniping is good press policy, too. In one daily paper several years ago, the recipe adopted was simple enough. Take six favourite figures in England today and break them. Nobody got lastingly broken, though the series was naturally a smash hit.

Certain pressmen and press-women carry an aura of self-importance suggesting a heavy sense of inferiority lurking below. I think these are the ones who can write (by no means a necessary qualification) and who are therefore still aware of the true value of words, aware how often they debase the currency. That, of course, is the trouble. Even the most embarrassing columnist must deal in words; respectable tools put here to a low purpose.

Humbert Wolfe wrote of Fleet Street:

Here they publish,
fresh and fresh,
news of the devil
and news of the flesh.
And as for the world,
they take the view
that it simply consists
of the other two.

And under the heading Talk-of-the-Devil I must stop to
note some illustrations of my theme as they appear in the
Daily Mail of today, September 8, 1960.

(i) Literary light from Tanfield's diary: *In a word, she
is the 67-year-old Mr Getty's solicitor.*

In *nine* words, dear boy.

(ii) Review of Noël Coward's latest play, a double column of the savagery to which the dramatist has long been
submitted. (Play still running as I correct these proofs.)
Large photograph carefully set across two neighbouring
columns shows Mr Coward in dinner-jacket, making a
speech on-stage with the cast behind him. Caption begins:
'The curtain has rung down on yet another Coward first
night.'

Mr Coward made no appearance at the London opening. The picture was taken in Dublin a month ago. I know
because I was there.

Even without malice aforethought the press of today
cannot—it seems—help making mistakes. Its readers are
bombarded with misstatements, inaccuracies, errors—not
only in taste as is to be expected—but errors in everything:
times, places and events all awry; names misspelled; a parade of blunders that could be saved so easily by checking.

130

The truth, as I have said, is not and cannot be the business of the journalist. But that simpler circumstance, the fact, *is* his business, and the basic tool of his trade. Strange that he so seldom makes use of it.

2

I have said that my integrity and I began as one; then split, in the normal process of growing up: so that I could look at it and it could look at me, neither of us always liking what we saw. The shadow-boxing bouts began. I can't remember when Integrity turned into Nanny for me. But she has been Nanny for years now, a stern abiding Nanny, who keeps particular watch on the money-making devices in the interim period between the novels: this is the time, in her view, when I am most liable to temptation. I know she is right, though I sometimes wish she would shut up.

On occasion I obey without a grumble, finding myself in complete agreement with her.

When I was young I heard talk of the 'modern girl' and the 'modern outlook'. I was the one, so presumably I had the other. No cause for alarm. In these days there is the same sort of talk, though the word used is not 'modern' but 'contemporary'. (Are all our words getting longer?) It is Nanny who reminds me that I cannot be 'contemporary'. Here I need no reminding.

My work is to observe, to understand, to reflect what I see and know. I am living through a part of the contemporary scene, but I must never stop to wonder if my view of it appears old-fashioned or out-of-date. To those who are young I cannot, surely, seem otherwise. And that is as it should be. No middle-aged writer need strive to keep up with the young literary Joneses. Their novels may be, and often are, better novels than he wrote in his twenties, but that's none of his business.

To aim at new fashions of thought, style and technique in the effort to seem 'contemporary' would be quite stupidly dishonest. I might as well try to fool myself that what I need to make me look more acceptable is a dress designed for a debutante. All that has gone to make up the middle-aged woman, spiritually, mentally, morally, is an accumulation of years and experiences. This must show in my books, as the lines show in my face, the wrinkles in my neck. The fifties are no time for *avant-garde* acrobatics, with an eye to new customers.

Do I imply, then, that I am now back where I was before the year 1929, blissfully unaware of the customers? No. For one thing, my work, my passion, has become a fairly profitable trade. (As Somerset Maugham says, quite a lot of people like to write books that quite a lot of people like to read.) If I were rich, would I just write and then put the books away in my desk? Of course I wouldn't. In common with other writers, I like to be read. But my unseen authority, that dim presence of whom I am sometimes aware when I work, cannot be called a customer. Whoever he may be, he has no face; he belongs to no category: he may be an imagined reader, but that's the most I can say in trying to identify him. If he were a customer I should be doing my best to give him what he wants on a basis of sound salesmanship and financial reward. This doesn't happen. I can't set out to give the customers what they want, for a variety of reasons, the most simple reason being that I haven't a clue what their wants are.

I believe that when a writer asks himself 'What do they

want?' he's bound to be in trouble. Not even the most skilled salesman can predict public taste with certainty. Which calls to mind an uncomfortable afternoon in the early Thirties.

The writer who was talking to me had written a number of good books before he hit the jackpot with a best-seller. A walloping best-seller. It had made headlines and a mint of money. Now, a year later, he was explaining the difficulties about writing his next. His face was solemn; his voice was hushed.

'One has to realise,' he said, 'that one is now quite a different person, with new, tremendous responsibilities.'

Humbly, I asked why. So did our hostess.

'My dears, can't you *see* why? Up till a year ago, when I was just struggling along, I was writing for myself; writing as I pleased. That's over. I don't belong to myself any more; I belong to *them*.'

Did we ask for further explanation? I don't remember: I know we got it: 'There's this whole vast public—waiting, waiting. I have a duty towards them, I mustn't let them down. They must have a book as good as the last,—if not better. That's their right.' He sighed. 'It's a *great* responsibility . . . If ever it happens to you' he added, 'you'll know what I mean.'

'Surely what he means,' I said after he left, 'is that he just wants to write another best-seller?'

'Well, yes, dear: and he's afraid he can't do it again.'

Crudely, I asked why he couldn't say so instead of wuffling on about duties and responsibility?

'Because he won't admit it, even to himself, don't you see? That's the way it takes people.'

I vowed furiously that it would never take me that way; that if ever I hit such a jackpot I wouldn't let it fool me into this kind of dishonesty. It's a vow I haven't yet needed to break: the occasion of sin has not arisen. When it does, if it does, I trust I'll know the symptoms by sight, diagnosing them more correctly as consciousness of the customers and the simple, wholly natural wish to get them buying again. I shall want to write another best-seller. And though I might try to do so, I think it would be difficult. Just as difficult, just as arbitrary, as to sit at my desk saying 'Now, by God, I'm going to write a book *nobody* will want to read.'

3

I was lately asked to give a lecture on the novel. I chose for my title: 'The Novelist: Artist or Tradesman?' When I received a copy of the leaflet announcing the lecture, I saw that the word 'Craftsman' had been substituted for 'Tradesman'. A covering letter said 'It was thought that the use of the word "Tradesman" might offend.'

Since I had just been making some nature-notes on the prevalence of umbrage, I was particularly interested. Who, in the audience, was likely to be offended—and why?

A novelist?

A tradesman?

Somebody of such refinement that any reference to tradesmen would be unbearable?

A subscriber to a lending-library who had always regarded the library as in some way superior to the grocer's and now wouldn't?

I gave it up. But the substitute title didn't seem to work. It made no argument. What was to prevent an artist from being a craftsman as well? Besides, I had intended no attack on tradesmen, nor indeed on artists. I was out to explore a part of the problem with which I ended my last chapter: the problem of being corruptible from the moment one puts pen to paper. I wanted to examine it from the angle of the professional.

The adjective 'professional' still stands as a compliment when applied to any skill outside the arts. Unprofessional symptoms in the work of lawyers, doctors, nurses or stockbrokers do not receive applause. But the book-reviewer, for example, has only to note that 'Miss Romp is of course a professional novelist and one cannot help admiring her adroit technique,' to sound as though it were all a sad pity. 'A smooth, professional job' implies that the novel isn't really worth reading.

And that brings me, if anything could, to the critics: on whom I expressed my views rather pompously for publication in *The Author* a year ago:

'The responsibilities of the reviewer of fiction are obvious. Even more obvious, in the year 1959, is the fact that he cannot live up to them. He earns far too little and he reads far too much. His space and his time are impossibly limited. Any novel worth reading must be read thoroughly and thoughtfully. Any novel worth reviewing must be dealt with at reasonable length. No reviewer with the current output of fiction on his hands and his current allowance of newsprint can be expected to do more than skip the book and sketch the gist of it.

'So he must manage as best he can. He will observe that certain jungle-laws have come into being and are now routine time-savers: for example the exhibition of prejudices and preconceived ideas: for example, the obligation to be as funny as possible about a bad book and to use a tone of throaty reverence for a good one. He can draw on the common stock of clichés:—"Lively", "Down-beat", "Readable", "Sincere", "Somehow Unsatisfactory" (no novel is ever "somehow satisfactory"), "It is a pity" and "Once again" . . .'

Referring to the denigration implicit in the adjective 'professional', I added 'Not long now, I think, before the verdict "Amateurish in every sense of the word" becomes the reviewer's highest praise,' and then summed up his duties as I saw them:

'A reviewer should remember that he is not a popular journalist, that a creative work is not as a rule a matter to be "written up" amusingly, personally or sensationally . . . He should be sparing with his stock of acids. This will come easier if he reminds himself regularly that here between these covers is the result of many months' deep thought and hard work . . . Should he find the book a loathsome failure, it is his duty to see that his attack is explicitly motivated and properly phrased. The light brush-off, the easy malice, the personal cracks, are no part of his job. I don't know how it ever came to be thought that they were. Not so long ago I attended a party where my hostess introduced "one of the youngest and cruellest of critics" as though she were paying the horrible child a pretty compliment.'

Well, it's all been said before, particularly by Jane Austen: '*Let us leave it to the reviewers to talk in threadbare strains of the trash with which the press now groans. Let us not desert one another: we are an injured body.*'

The reviewer is the picador, the writer the wounded bull. And so it will go on. And I do not approve and I am not resigned, but the fight itself can be fun.

It was, I think, in the year 1934 that Mr Cecil King decided to inaugurate a regular book-page in the *Daily Mir-*

ror. I was one of the candidates for the job. I had done no reviewing to date and this sounded as though it might be a challenge, until Mr King said: 'There's only one stipulation I want you to bear in mind: apart from that, you can write exactly as you please; no holds barred.'

I asked what the stipulation was. It was, he said, merely a matter of phrasing, though an important matter. For the purpose of this page, the resident reviewer must be forthright and direct. He or she must never say 'In my opinion this is the best book of the year.' He must come out unequivocally with: 'This *is* the best book of the year.' He must deal similarly with writers. 'There's no doubt who's the best writer in England today' he added . . 'Goes without saying . . . Beverley Nichols.'

I didn't get the job. It was awarded to one of the few critics who ever spent fifteen minutes apologising torrentially in the tube for the vicious notice she had given me. Station after station went by. At last I managed to get a word in. 'I'm sorry,' I said, 'but I've been abroad for weeks and I only got back yesterday, so I haven't seen your notice.' She cut it out and sent it to me.

While reading for the Book Society I was obliged to write reviews regularly: since I was one of the committee who chose the books, it was axiomatic that what I wrote would be favourable. No obligation to cut and thrust. Even so, after a very few weeks, I was saddened to find myself slipping into the traditional reviewer's idiom, the *de-haut-en-bas* idiom that I find so poisonous. Even in praising a novel, I discovered, I was beginning to make myself sound as though I could have written it as well—or better. I pressed on for a year, but it was a relief, once I had resigned, to be free of the mysterious disease, Critic's Sniff.

In New York ten years ago, my favourite and least popular novel was turned down by my publisher: an awkward circumstance all round. It was the first book on a three-book contract: I was drawing a regular salary. The publisher would have liked to like it. But he couldn't. Nor could anyone else in the office. They even tried the head of the sales-department, just in case . . . Finally they decided to invite an impartial opinion from a critic who had shown interest in my work.

Later on I was allowed to read his letter. He had obviously taken trouble. He made a thorough and thoughtful appraisal. Though he took the majority view, many of his comments were kind enough. No writer in his senses could have been hurt by these opinions, even though they added up to an adverse notice. The letter, to my astonishment, ended 'If I reviewed it, I am afraid I should have to be caustically severe.'

'Have to be,' eh? Yes, I see why; in the picador tradition, among the enduring germs of Critic's Sniff, one 'has to be' caustically severe.

Equally of course, there have to be book-reviews, just as there have to be things like the laundry and early closing. And at least a book is not in peril from the critics, as a play is in peril. A play can be killed. The book will still be there when the chorus of abuse has died down.

Why so much talk of bad reviews? Does it seem disingenuous? Do I sound as self-deceiving as the man who really just wanted to write another best-seller? Perhaps . . . You may well have concluded by now that the guinea-pig for this part of the experiment is coming up with an easily recognisable symptom: that of loving her good reviews and hating her bad ones.

But if you have so decided, I am afraid you are wrong.

I no longer read my reviews at all. This habit has grown upon me gradually. It began to form six years ago.

I had come in, on an early autumn evening, to the furnished flat where I lived alone. The mat inside the front door was strewn with plump little packets and long yellow envelopes. All the English press-cuttings and all the American press-cuttings seemed to have arrived at once. The novel had been a Book Society Choice in England; it was to be found on the best-seller lists in America. I myself rather liked it.

Having nothing better to do, I took the whole consignment with me to a comfortable chair. I decided to go through the lot. Some I had seen already; about two-thirds were new to me. The task took me more than an hour. This mainly because the American reviewer is not hampered for space and likes to tell the story of the book (thus proving he's read it, a phenomenon that surprised me considerably when it first came my way.) On and on I went. For many years it had been my habit to sniff delicately at my notices and throw away the bad ones as soon as I saw the line they were taking. Not now. I hardly skipped a word.

It appeared on the whole to be a favourable press, particularly in America. I should have been pleased. I wasn't displeased. I simply and suddenly realised I was boring myself to death. I couldn't go on reading. I didn't care. This realisation brought a sense of guilt. A moment later, with the furtive gesture of a child doing something naughty, I threw the whole lot into the wastepaper basket. They filled it quite full.

I stood there remembering the splendid press-cutting book that my mother and I had bought together at Windsor in 1927. I hadn't set eyes on the book for many years.

The Lord only knew what happened to it. Intermittently I had struggled to hoard a selection of good notices in an envelope (and the Lord only knew what happened to all the envelopes . . .)

Still feeling guilty, I cooked my dinner. I tried to establish reasons why reviews, good or bad, should have become a burden. Had I just eaten too many at a time? Perhaps. It seemed the simplest solution.

There were further instalments of press-cuttings on that book and I skipped through them, finding it hard to concentrate. One thing I realised was that even the favourable ones were affecting me as personal remarks sometimes affect me: making me feel crowded, subject to intrusion, claustrophobic. And another thing: when reviewers praised the book, they seemed to praise it for all the wrong reasons.

This ungrateful attitude survived the last of those particular press-cuttings.

I didn't publish another novel for nearly three years because I was trying to write for the theatre—a beguiling but unprofitable side-step. When the next book came out, I read three reviews by mistake, opening the newspapers before I saw them coming. I didn't touch the press-cuttings. Nor have I since. And now when my eyes catch sight of a review in the paper I turn the page. In this regard, I think I have come to resemble somebody who has no sense of smell, oblivious to the delights of Arpège along with the unwelcome signal from a bad egg.

How many writers contract this symptom in their middle years—or before? I should like to know. And I should like to know if they meet with the same disbelief. It is hard to persuade anybody that I am telling the truth when I say I do not, and do not want to, read my notices. I still receive those gleefully-tinted commiserations on a bad press. Friends still try to quote (from good and bad alike) down the telephone; or cut them out and send them: or kindly sum up the general trend of them in a précis of the reactions I have deliberately avoided. And, in spite of my cries, one or another publisher will sooner or later send me a fat bunch of reviews, all carefully collected from publication-day onwards. Over to the wastepaper basket again . . .

4

And here we are at money. I seem to have kept it hanging around this chapter without letting it take stage-centre.

My attitude towards money is ambivalent and has been this way ever since the year 1929 robbed me of my innocence. I am devoted to money. I like having enough to make it unnecessary to think once, let alone twice, about cashing a cheque. I like to pay my bills punctually. I like giving money to people, and buying things, and many of the things I buy must rate as luxuries, the things that do not endure: restaurant-dinners, taxis, flowers, first-class travel, bath-essence, chips to put on the roulette-table. Such solvency as I have attained has come more by good luck than good management. My congenital gambling instinct bolsters my belief that it will last—or that, if it doesn't, something will turn up.

Though I have never been nearly as big a best-seller as some people believe me to be, I have earned a good deal of money. I have spent it as it came. I have never learned to handle it sensibly and I doubt I ever shall. My beginnings saw to that. Looking back at my youth, I can see how those years were dominated by debt. Why that happened and went on happening is simple enough. Two-thirds of the bills I took it upon myself to owe, and finally to pay, were not my own.

I paid my mother's bills and my aunts' bills and my grandmother's bills and my cousin-in-law's bills and in due course my husband's bills; as well as the bills of many people who were not related to me at all. At intervals, as a result of this psychotic procedure, somebody else paid mine and had to be paid back.

Sometimes I have been the victim of my own weakness; sometimes of emotional pressure from without. There is another side to it: the 'I'll pay' frenzy that takes me unawares, making me grab the bill out of the waiter's hand while all those present register their sincere protests. From what Freudian depths these glad, forceful cries of 'This is on me . .' come up, I'll never know. They did me no good when I was young.

Youth, I see, would have been a fine affair but for debts and spots. The debts, like the spots, have left some lasting scars.

There are those who can live happily insolvent all their lives. There are those who need to save to feel safe. And there are those like myself: who cannot live happily insolvent and still find difficulty in asking the question 'Can I afford it?' without answering promptly 'Of course.'

I confess these confusions because they help to account for my seeing the professional novelist as a person in a dilemma. I meet few who agree. When I said on a public platform lately, 'There's no steady living to be made writing novels' I was contradicted by two known and successful writers, a man and a woman. Both could claim that they had made a steady living for themselves and their families.

What I meant was that without the incidental jackpots (movie-rights, dramatic rights, American serial-rights, softcovers, Books of the Month and the rest) a novel alone could not pay the writer's way. But the overtone, I think, was that I, being the kind of person I am, could never rely on making a regular income out of anything. And I kept something else unsaid; this: that one oughtn't to rely on the regular income anyway, lest one be in danger of making sales and customers the target. (By 'one' I mean me again). Wonderful when the cash comes in, or the bitch-goddess smiles, but that's not the object of the exercise: it mustn't be.

At the stage where creative restlessness lies dead, the stage wherein I'm waiting impatiently upon the next idea, I am not saying to myself 'Hurry up, now, and earn some money.' On the other hand I have often looked at my shrinking bank-balance and said 'If you don't get an idea soon you're going to be in trouble'—and been in it. The difference between these two angles may seem small. But as far as I'm concerned it sums up the dilemma.

Once the idea has brought the impulse back, I am artist, craftsman, tradesman all in one. Would I be a better artist if nobody had ever bought a book of mine? I don't know. Would I be a more successful tradesman if I really liked writing for money instead of writing for its own sake? I couldn't say at all.

But I know this: the important thing for me, always, has been to go on, to keep at it; not to let the slack periods, the interim dryness nor even the well-earned holiday rust the tools. They rust all too easily.

I have believed for many years that there is a special

devil—or maybe a whole corps of them—deputed to thwart creative work simply because it is creative. To any writer who is setting out I would say Beware the pause that lasts too long. Even if you're rich enough for it not to matter, it still does matter. The only way to learn to write well is to keep writing: the only way to safeguard the talent is to exercise it. And that means keeping the door of your room shut and working alone. Outside the door there may be the beguiling band-wagon noises or the hollow silence of apparent defeat. Neither, as you work, is your concern. Your concern is with a gift and the service of it. Given the ready ear, the open eye, the purpose and the stamina, you will not be safe, because nobody can be safe. But you will be armed.

CHAPTER
SEVEN

1

My last appearances as guinea-pig will be made, as you might say, in a Transatlantic laboratory. Any English writer who knows America and has sold his work there must find the continent as fascinating—and possibly as puzzling—as I find it.

Between the Americans and the British (I have said this before) there exists a profound natural antipathy, as between dogs and cats. Certainly there are dogs who love cats, and cats who get on fine with dogs. I have also in my time known a cat who was terrified of cats and a dog who simply hated dogs. But these are exceptions. And sufferers from Transatlantic schizophrenia (whether like myself they come from England and love America, or vice versa) remain a minority.

Having lived for ten years in the United States, I am now as a cat who has learned to love, and live among, dogs. Yet in America I still meet many a dog who sees me for what I am, a cat, and shows the normal dog's reaction. It was on Long John's radio-programme in New York that I began to ask my neighbour 'What do you like about the British something-or-other?' (Whether we were

145

discussing literature, politics, food or scenery I have forgotten . . .) I didn't get to the noun because he cut me off automatically with 'Heck, I don't like *anything* about the British.' (Heck is the mandatory substitute for Hell on the air.)

When I have been on the American side for a while, I unconsciously acquire certain dog-qualities which make me, on my return to England, a little suspect and estranged among my fellow cats.

The difference between us is very deep. To me it defies a neat analysis, a clear exposition. All the obvious differences are there on the surface: looks, language, manners, habits. I was quite sure when I first arrived in New York that the surface could be discounted. When I got to know them, I said, I should find the same sort of animals as myself. And I got to know them and saw I was quite wrong.

Few things, to a writer, could have been more frustrating. Here I was; possessed of a whole country, a whole new crowd of people, yet defeated in my task of getting under the American skin, writing over the American shoulder. I had found them, but I didn't understand them. So I couldn't be an American on paper. Writing of them I had to write mostly from the outside, looking at them through the eyes of English characters. I made brief excursions into their heads—darting out again as soon as possible. Gradually, of course, I drew closer to the different animals. Slowly I began to be them. But I had spent five years among them before I could really write 'with ease and affection' from the American point of view.

'Why? Where's the difference? Never aware of it in my life,' said the ex-Rhodes scholar, now a professor at Stanford University: 'We're the same animal as you.'

'Didn't you feel any difference when you first went to Oxford?'

No, he hadn't. On the contrary. At Oxford he had understood his best friend well enough to write all his love-letters for him. (I sometimes wish we had pursued this conversation further . . .) In his view, I was merely homesick, fresh from wartime Europe and over-critical.

One of my in-laws asked me why my books didn't dig deeper into the emotions of the American woman. She, like the Rhodes scholar, protested that the difference existed only in my imagination.

I find, from a table of comparisons made not long ago:

AMERICANS: Slow.

ENGLISH: Quicker.

AMERICANS: Wary of what they don't understand.

ENGLISH: Skip what they don't understand.

AMERICANS: Endless curiosity and sympathy in individual human beings, hampered only by lack of imagination.

ENGLISH: No curiosity; sympathetic interest in the individual confined to minding other people's business. Strong in imagination.

AMERICAN MEN: Like women, and fear them.

ENGLISHMEN: Dislike women and don't fear them.

AMERICANS: Blaspheme.

ENGLISH: Swear.

AMERICANS: Passionate for physical health: take endless trouble to avoid death.

ENGLISH: Find ill-health not only interesting but respectable and often experience death in the effort to avoid a fuss.

147

Which doesn't really get us far, but proves I'm still working at it. Incidentally, none of the above notations apply to any American or English friend of mine and correspondence is not encouraged.

2

'No, no, put it back—it's American,' said a sharp female voice in my ear. The place was the Times Bookshop and I was loitering beside the new thrillers, taking my pick. So was the owner of the sharp female voice. Her friend, in acquiescent, understanding haste, returned the book to the stack. They moved on, searching out English titles. I, who find the Americans especially adept in the art of the thriller, looked at them moodily, wondering whether to weigh in. They were missing a lot. Did I care?

Well yes, I did care, though I didn't tell them so. None of my business, I thought as I twitched the latest Helen McGloy from its place; but need they be so bloody patronising? It is the patronage of the English when they imitate an American accent—which, unaccountably, they feel compelled to do whenever the opportunity occurs.

I don't know how many different sorts of American accent there are: I should guess at least twenty-five, and unless one has a highly-trained ear they are extremely difficult to reproduce. When the English relay American talk, they have to put the accent in. At least that is the intention. What happens is a peculiar nasal sing-song and a liberal sprinkling of expressions like 'Gee', 'Say', 'Mebbe', 'I guess', 'I reckon' and 'Gonna'. 'Doesn't matter whether they are quoting a Senator, a Middle West matron, a Vanderbilt, a Bostonian, a Southern belle or a negro, the imitation is inevitably the same, inevitably excruciating.

This misapprehension can be found in most English novels where Americans are portrayed. The dialogue makes painful reading. And there is little excuse for it. The idiom can be checked with one of the simple natives—a precaution I have learned to take.

American is a subtle language, harder to learn than French because it starts with a misleading likeness to our own and develops differences at once. After you have lived over there for a while you begin to speak it naturally and to lose your ear for the small but important differences.

When John van Druten's play *Bell, Book and Candle* was to be produced in London, he sent me a copy of the script. In his letter he told me that the play would be anglicised throughout; all the characters British, the setting transposed from New York to London: 'You're the only person I know who still knows both languages well enough to vet the dialogue thoroughly and advise on changes. I've made quite a few, so this is the purported English version. But I don't trust my ear after living so long on this side.'

He enclosed a cheque, though I would have done the job for love and my own amusement. I went through the script assiduously, finding on almost every page a line that needed translation: 'I'll stop by', 'Some place else', 'You don't say?' and such. Where I failed the author was in finding an English substitute, or even a parallel, for 'Double-header'. (Any offers?) Writing to acknowledge my list, he said 'I'd already taken out a hundred and twenty before the script went to you.'

Back in London for a brief stay, the following year, I lunched with a magazine-editor who wanted a short story. I had one in mind: the sort of story you can tell, as Alexander Korda said, on an aspirin-tablet. I told it to the editor: she liked it. 'But *must* it have an American background? We simply can't use American stories any more: the life on both sides is so utterly different since the war.'

I thought about this. I had planned to write the story for the American market. But it might just as well be English. Neither the situations nor the characters were exclusively American. How would it be to write the story twice —first in one language, then in the other? I was between novels, therefore between cheques. This could, I thought, be an instructive as well as a profitable ploy. It wouldn't take me long.

Next day I began; with the English version. There were only two scenes throughout; for Greenwich Village and Connecticut I substituted Chelsea and Sussex. I was half-way through when my sister came home from work. She asked to read it. No; it was all scribbles, it was still in the Rough, but I would, I said, read it to her. (Since as I have observed elsewhere, the human race consists entirely of those who like to read aloud and those who hate to be read aloud to, it is remarkable that any reading aloud gets done. With a sigh and her knitting, my sister capitulated.)

When I had finished, she said 'I thought you were going to start with the English version?'

'This is the English version.'

She blinked. Chelsea, I said; Sussex, I pointed out.

'Yes, I know. But you're writing pure American; all your characters are talking like Americans. If I read it in a magazine I'd think it was an anglicised version,—the sort you used to do for *Woman's Journal.*'

Re-reading, I saw she was right. I had temporarily lost the trick of writing true English. I went over to the American version. I never could sell the story in U.S.A. but presently a London magazine bought it and changed the background.

3

The American market remains a mystery to most English readers, including me. There are many writers who do well enough here—and make no impact there. But the trick isn't a matter of knowing the country or the American *ethos*. On the contrary. Novelists who write exclusively of Europe and have never been near America can sell their thousands on the other side. Though, by the way, the famous 'best-seller lists' in the *New York Times* and *Tribune* are something of a delusion. Novels sell in smaller quantities there than here. (Except, of course, the Book Club choices and that curious American blend of bare bosoms, history, sex and swashbuckle, set anywhere from Jerusalem, 30 A.D. to South Carolina 1880.)

I have not yet solved the market-mystery. And for me the American novel is almost always too long, too detailed and too slow. Yet I have heard American publishers complain that the British novel, though well-written, lacks action: 'Not enough happens; no suspense; all talky-talk—you know?'

No, I don't know. I am devoted, as anybody who has read thus far must realise, to the photographic method, the visual scene. But a prolonged indulgence of camera-work when nothing much is going on can be lethal in its effect; and this I find particularly an American vice. I mean the deadpan slow-motion technique that records, for example, every stage in the progress of a man waking up, climbing out of bed, taking his shower, brushing his teeth, shaving, dressing and getting his breakfast. By the time he has broken those two eggs into the knob of butter that's melting in the deadpan—sorry, skillet—my feeling is that midnight will strike any minute now.

I realise that food plays a highly important part in American fiction, just as it does in American daily life. (Over there, I can get indigestion merely by reading a dinner-menu or a full-page advertisement for cooked ham.) In California in 1948 I was writing a short story aimed on the American magazine-market. I was fond of this story: the idea was, I thought, good enough to keep old Nanny Integrity in an amiable temper and earn me some badly-needed money meanwhile. Looking through the Rough, I was taken with a sudden attack of huckster's insight: 'Goodness,' I said to myself, 'there ought to be some food in it somewhere.' At once I knew where; and what. A few days before, I had made cream buns/cream puffs (cross out one) for the first time. The angst and the ecstasy still haunted me. 'That'll send them,' I said, with a quick glance at Nanny to make sure she was still asleep. When she opened her eyes and glared, I pleaded 'Look . . it's not badly written and it's *true*.' Resigned, she nodded off again.

Cosmopolitan bought the story for eight hundred and fifty dollars, and all the bells rang out as I read my agent's telegram. Would I, the telegram asked, agree to a two-thousand word cut? I wired back 'Tell them they can cut the whole story for that price.' Then there was some discussion about the title. I had called it 'Second Chance'. My agent did better with 'Cellini and the Cream Puffs' until somebody pointed out (news to me) that cream puff was American for homosexual. The story finally appeared as 'This Was Love' and the two-thousand word cut removed the cooking sequence altogether.

152

My efforts to woo the magazine-editors continued, in spite of Nanny, for five more years. I was so short of money that when there wasn't a novel about I could only see this gold-mine beckoning and try to dig. One woman editor told me I needed a stronger story-line but wouldn't agree that 'plot' was what she meant, at the same time refusing to give another definition. The next editor I met was a man. I was writing a thirty-thousand word serial that had begun as an idea for a movie-script. My private life was in pieces; there was no novel in sight; Nanny and I had practically ceased to be on speaking-terms. But my agent had said this might make a 'long-shot' so I met the editor.

'It doesn't,' he said kindly, 'have to be that long.'

'Well, that's the way it looks to me.'

He assured me that ten thousand words would be enough for his purposes and laughingly discounted the needs of mine. We were not really getting on very well. When we parted he picked up two sets of galleys, new novels to read on his commuter's journey home. Since the journey took only an hour and a quarter I asked more about this. He had, he said, perfected a reading method by which he skipped the first and the last word of every line:

'Makes no difference to the sense. I find I can leave 'em out every time. It's a technique I taught myself a long while ago and now I just never read them.'

I said 'Well in that case, surely, I need never write them?' but he didn't agree.

I wrote my thirty thousand words. The editor of *Ladies Home Journal* said I was cynically pulling the leg of the great American public. No other editor said anything except No. It was sold twice for T.V. in New York and once as a serial in Australia.

Here is a log of my short-story progress in U.S.A.

1930 (*a*) A long sad one about my first love, rejected by all the English magazines, bought by *Cosmopolitan*, paid for on the nail and never, to my knowledge, published.

(*b*) A short funny one, rejected by all the English magazines, bought and published by the *Chicago Tribune*.

1930–1936 No sale.

1937 'Could you' asked my London agent over the telephone 'write a short story called Wedding Week-End?' He sounded as though he had giggles. I was in the middle of a book. I said I supposed I could, though such a thought had not occurred to me.

'*Woman's Journal* are running a "Brides" number—just going to press; they chose this title for a story they commissioned; now they've got the story they don't like it, so they're in a jam.'

'When do they want it?'

'Monday.'

'Good God, it's Thursday now.'

'Precisely. They'll pay thirty guineas.'

'All right' I said, 'I'll oblige.'

I met the deadline. *Woman's Journal* said my 'Wedding Week-End' was cynical and unusable. I said it was neither. On the other hand it was a commission and I had lost a good deal of sleep, as well as valuable time on my novel. They paid up, with those two peculiar editorial provisos: one, that I should offer them my next story in lieu; or, two, that if I sold it elsewhere I should pay them back. In a remarkably short time an American magazine whose name escapes me paid a hundred guineas for it and I refunded *W.J.*

1937–1940 No sale.

154

1940 Ten short stories written for the American market, local idiom and background carefully checked, while I waited to get back to England and the war. None sold there. Nine of them sold in England, with local idiom and background carefully removed. Number Ten sold in Canada.

1941 *Woman's Journal* suddenly sent me an American story to anglicise. It was a war story, set in an English village where a German spy was dropped by parachute. Most of the action took place in a pub. My favourite character was rather perplexingly referred to as The Lord. The Lord sat at a separate table from the rest, drinking from a cobwebbed bottle of brandy. He was jolly sporting at the darts-game.

1940–1946 No sale.

1946 Nearly sold a piece to *Reader's Digest,* for 'Drama in Everyday Life' series. Rejection-letter said the editor particularly admired the Double Gag in the Last Canto. Regretfully though, he told me that Americans would be distressed to read about an unnatural mother. He enclosed a list of human qualities suitable for the series. The list included courage, kindliness, loyalty, integrity (Why, Nanny!) and self-sacrifice.

1946–1947 Many stories, no sale.

1948 Cream Puffs, as noted.

1948–1950 No sale.

1951 Story, deliberately aimed, sold to *Collier's* who paid eleven hundred dollars by return.

4

The acceptance by *Collier's* marked a turning-point; though not the kind of turning-point one usually reads about in success-stories. Once the cheque landed I was drunk with power. The story wasn't a masterpiece; nor was it one to be ashamed of. I remember thinking that I had, at last, got the trick and found the gold.

I was on Martha's Vineyard that summer, in a small rented cottage, where I planned to begin my next novel. The novel had hung around for three years and I was anxious to get on. But this eleven-hundred bonus gave me pause for reflection. Surely I could do that again, just once. . .

I set out with a French Riviera background, a delinquent boy, a moody girl and a kind wise father who acted villain throughout until proved a saint in the last sequence. Nanny however, woke up just as I'd finished the Rough and consigned the whole thing to the trash-basket. She allowed that there was something reputable about the beginning. I brooded on the beginning.

At the end of two weeks I had written what seemed to me a very peculiar tale. Instead of the required five thousand words I had written about thirteen thousand. I called it 'The Moon, the Duchess and the Other People'. It was obviously unsaleable and I liked it better than anything I had done in years. The characters, rather disturbingly, stuck around; haunting me as they do when I haven't really finished a book,—the sure sign of trouble somewhere.

Turning my back on them, I took a running dive into the novel. All that summer, autumn, and most of the winter, my peculiar story was going the rounds. No and No and No. *Ladies Home Journal* looked for a moment as though it might accept, but the top brass gave as their ruling that the story was subversive and un-American. Finally my agent, having exhausted the well-paying 'Slicks' sent it to *Harper's Magazine.* They paid five hundred dollars. Under the title 'The Duchess and the Smugs,' this story has made more money for me than any other single work in my life. It gave me something of a name in America. It became the first part of a novel; it was a Ford Foundation television play; it dealt me the jackpot with its publication in *Reader's Digest* Quarterly Books.

There's a puzzle here: a puzzle that relates to the mystery already mentioned. The characters were English: the background was French; not a whisper of American was to be heard. Yet its whole success was made in the United States. I had fan-letters from all over the continent. I still get them occasionally now, eight years after.

5

Quoting poetry, as Evelyn Waugh and others have indicated, is an English vice. I have this vice. When I indulge it outside literary circles in U.S.A., I am usually asked to repeat what I have just said.

I repeat: '"The gods are just, and of our pleasant vices make instruments to plague us . . ."'

An awed look comes into the eyes: 'Why, that's a very wonderful way you have of expressing it.'

'Not so much me as William Shakespeare.'

''Mean it's a quotation?'

'Yes.'

'What a memory you must have.'

I still indulge the vice in every novel I write, though I really don't know how I have any quotations left after the book called *The Willow Cabin*—which was peppered with them from start to finish. Since I had put in every one from memory I had a busy time checking them. I was living in California and sources were hard to come by. But for Charles Abbott and the Lockwood Memorial Library, Buffalo, I could never have run them all to earth before the English proofs arrived. These found me deep in humiliation. At least eighty per cent were badly misquoted, and as they were all old favourites it appeared I had been misquoting for about twenty-five years.

The English proof, heavily bespeckled, had just been dispatched when the American galleys turned up. I wasn't expecting them so soon. They were wanted back in a hurry. 'Don't worry about the quotations,' the editor told me, 'the main reason for these galleys is that we still need a few cuts. You'll be getting page-proofs later on.'

What I got later on was a bound copy. It looked very pretty from the outside, but all the misquotations were still inside; including quite a new one, the printer's own, sitting among the various lines from 'Twelfth Night' with which I had introduced each section of the book.

I rushed screaming to the telephone and called New York. Everybody was very sorry and nothing could be done. Fifteen hundred copies were in print. An erratum slip was suggested. (I have been fond of these ever since I found one in Strachey's *Elizabeth and Essex,* which included the correction 'For sex read Essex.') Then it was decided not to use the erratum slip for fear of drawing attention to the errata. All the reviewers got these shaming copies; they had to; I didn't draw an easy breath till Au-

158

gust when the first review came out with 'Pamela Frankau has taken her title from "The Tempest" '—and I felt much, much better. So did the editor.

Editors, now . . . *There's* a thing, as we used to say in the army. I regard the editorial function in the American publishing-house with increasing dismay. The editor is one symbol of the accepted committee-work done nowadays on a novel—to its detriment. I grant that all writers should have the courtesy to listen to queries or criticisms from the publisher. I grant also that some of these may be valid. And that, I fear, is where the granting has to stop.

There are some highly dangerous misapprehensions among American editors and if they go on this way they are liable to kill off their authors young. (In fact the effects of the well-intentioned homicide are already visible.)

It's quite easy to see how this happens. An editor whose function it is to make suggestions for improvement rapidly acquires the habit of seeing every novel, not as a finished product but as a basis for discussion; not as its author's property but as a shared venture. He approaches the work in a mood of urbane authority—in a hearty, kindly 'Let's-see-what-has-to-be-done' frame of mind. The menace to a young writer is considerable. One or another of these semi-literary figures takes him over, body and soul. He turns into a pupil with a cosy, knowing teacher. The editor makes regular enquiries after the work in progress; he expects to see and discuss the half-finished product (to my mind a fatally inept procedure.) When he sees it, he comes up with criticisms and suggestions. In other words he is forcing the study door and breathing heavily down the writer's neck. Small wonder that so many of the younger ones desert the desk for the analyst's couch.

It was a young one, with a remarkable first novel to his

credit, who shook me by asking 'What *sort* of corrections should an editor make on the draft one sends him?'

'None,' I snapped.

He placed in my hands a typescript scored with little marks, down the margin and along the tops of the lines. There were dozens of them.

'Did you say this was a first draft?'

'Yes: the first six chapters.'

'What on earth made you send it to him?'

'He asked to see it.'

'Even so—did you want him to see it?'

'Kind of . . I wasn't too happy about the beginning. I wanted *somebody* to take a look.'

This temptation, I explained in an auntlike way, comes to all of us. It may come from a lonely lack of confidence, or from a purr of pride. No matter which, the end-product is the same. What we want is approval. We feel the need for praise or at the least, reassurance, before we go on.

'You are therefore,' I intoned, 'something of a sitting duck for editorial interference, are you not?'

'Yes. But you see, the editor's work—'

—'The editor's work is to kill off geese who might otherwise lay golden eggs, in my view. Your book at this stage is your business, not his.'

I don't know if he kept his door shut after that; but he finished his novel. Too many of his kind, full of talent, write a first novel and then fade away because the anxiety of committee-work and pleasing teacher prove too much for them. Some useful directions for beginners in *The Manual of Style,* Chicago University Press, are presented under the heading 'How to Win a Publisher'. I wish the Manual would include some directions for publishers under the heading 'How to Treat an Author'.

The current mistaken method owes itself, I believe, to two factors; one psychological and the other financial. The American disease of 'insecurity' drives authors to seek the shelter of the editorial wing. The high overhead costs in the business drive the publisher to take every frenzied measure he can to ensure a saleable book. Jackpot or nothing is the trouble. A New York publisher told me two years ago that he had one great envy of the English publisher: 'He can still afford to take a chance on a new author. He can buy a novel that won't sell more than two thousand copies because he believes in the writer's future. We can't do that. It's too expensive. I know we make plenty of mistakes, but what we have to aim at every time is a big sale. Before the war there was such a thing as a "publishable" book; a losing investment, maybe, but worthwhile in itself and an act of faith in the future. Not now. Not any more. It's a bad risk.'

Victor Gollancz, over in New York to buy American fiction, was shocked when the editors in one house told him of the alterations they had asked the novelist to make. He had already bought the book and he wanted it the way it was. He protested vociferously. The answer was 'Artistically of course you're right. But we're hoping to get a really big sale with this one.'

It was Mr Gollancz who told me to keep a wary eye on the copy-editor, because he was empowered to make alterations even when the author had passed the final proof. It was a very young, very angry, very intelligent New York publisher who attacked me for attacking the copy-editor.

'He's invaluable. No house could do without him.'

'Well, all right. Just so's he doesn't jigger about with the book on his own account.'

'But he has to. What else can he do with some of the illiterate stuff we handle?'

'Surely if people are illiterate they can't be writers.'

'You come from England,' he said, as though that settled it.

In America, as here, I deplore the accepted use of the ghost-writer. Public characters of all shapes and sizes, who cannot put pen to paper, now put their names to books: a prank which must make any professional shudder.

The ghost writer, by the way, is about the only ghost in whom the American believes. This is understandable. For belief in ghosts you need either imagination or actual experience. Imagination isn't a national strong point; experience seems to be lacking. (The only ghost I ever saw in America was a Red Indian, a black cut-out figure, like Peter Pan's shadow, moving across a river-mist at Rhinebeck.) The supernatural remains at a heavy discount in U.S.A. Here a fragment of conversation occurs to mind. My lunch-time neighbour turned to me, saying suddenly 'We had a British novelist visit us last week. He told me there was a ghost in his house, back home.'

She was obviously poised for a laugh, so I thought it was going to be a funny ghost. I waited for the point of the story. Presently I became aware that this was the point of the story: I was expected to laugh. The American is as credulous as the Englishman in accepting the claims of high-powered advertising, newspaper reports, defence-estimates, wonder-drugs and the rest. But the notion of a world beyond is usually beyond him. Religion, of course, in bewildering variety. But nothing as non-conformist as a phantom.

6

A Stanford student once read himself to sleep with the dictionary, the aim being to learn at least five new words a night. I could have kissed him. Heaven alone knew what he would do with them when he had mastered them. Americans treat their language with a furiously abundant energy —contriving two words for the price of one, hooking up unlikely neighbours with a hyphen, turning nouns into verbs and verbs into nouns—and generally beating the hell out of it. This Let's-have-a-word-picnic instinct is sometimes fortunate in its results, sometimes unfortunate. Here at least, in the Stanford student, was somebody who cared about the possession of a vocabulary.

We, the English, do not care. We hug our laziness about our language. We neither know its scope nor think to explore it. A Frenchman, as he talks, enjoys words, enjoys making them work for him. An American, wildly coining the most hideous expressions, is at least having a bash. We don't even try. Despite our heritage we keep our puritanical distrust of eloquence. 'A man of few words' has become a high compliment, though in my experience he often proves equally short of ideas. Because we have no respect for articulacy we have become the worst listeners in the world. Does any other nation say 'Pardon—' 'What?' and 'I didn't quite catch—' with such automatic, assured regularity? Not answering at all is a favourite English sport. This may in part be due to the fact that we are so difficult to hear; we like to mumble. Possibly something to do with keeping a stiff upper lip.

When first in America I was surprised by the precision

of speech. 'What-d'you-call-it' and 'Thingummy' were mysteriously absent. When an introduction was made, the name was clearly pronounced.

That we should so purposely impoverish, so devoutly limit, our everyday language is all the odder since we have poetry in us and can, as in 1940, respond to great words.

But, Lord have mercy, look at the words we respond to without complaint. Why do we never revolt against the continual spate of bleak insults offered us in public places? The eternal, dictatorial 'No' confronts us everywhere. No smoking; no cheques cashed; no entry; no dogs; no meals served after ten p.m.; no parking; no admittance . . no this, no that, and no the other thing: topping up with my favourite: CAMDEN TOWN; NO ACCIDENTS, PLEASE. (Well, at least it says 'please', a courtesy to the millions who enjoy accidents and need urging to lay off this luxurious addiction while driving through Camden Town.)

I should like to lead a crusade against the dictatorial negative. Necessary regulations should be rewritten in the politer positive: *Cheques will be cashed, subject to three days' notice. Meals will be served up till ten p.m.* The unnecessary strictures can be abolished altogether. Let us find out as we go along. The fact, for example, that an hotel-management WILL NOT BE RESPONSIBLE FOR . . . doesn't need to yell at us from a framed manifesto on the wall. When we've been robbed, we'll know.

In America there is rather less of the No and some rather exaggerated attempts to be jolly, such as heralding obstructive road-works with the news that 'Massachusetts is forging yet another new link in its vast network of public highways' and putting up a sign saying 'Thank you for your co-operation' when you have driven, having no alternative, through the worst of the shambles. WE LOVE OUR

CHILDREN is an extension of the No-accidents-please idea. It means Don't run over them. On the whole I'd say the American sign-writer sets out to woo us; sometimes too threateningly, as in the restaurant where there was a notice on the wall saying 'We'll be real sore if you don't ask for a second serving.'

The menu is a persistent wooer; it can sometimes remove the appetite altogether: SIZZLING HAM-STEAK AND TWO EGGS, COUNTRY FARMHOUSE STYLE: CRISPY CRUNCHY CEREAL WITH THICK RICH CREAM: GOLDEN FRENCH FRIED POTATOES: PLUMP SWEET JUICY GARDEN PEAS. THE HAMBURGER IS SERVED IN A HUGE TOASTED BUN.

Make mine a brandy.

CHAPTER
EIGHT

1

My nature-notes on umbrage seem to prove that the British kind and the American kind have some differences, as might be expected. It was in the year 1949 that I managed, in a small way, to attract both. It is a sad story. 1947–1949 was my period of trying to dig gold from the American market. During this time I came to know and love the country, to look upon California as a pleasant place to live. But as a prophet I remained a dead loss on my home ground. (The novel that began to change all that was still with the printers.) I had offered myself as a lecturer and broadcaster in San Francisco, without success. My name meant nothing, the authorities explained patiently; nobody knew it. Always a bad salesman, with little talent for publicity, I stayed shrouded.

At the end of July '49, I sailed for England. Here the novel was already out and doing well. I was basking under sunshine and solvency in Devonshire when the *Evening Standard* asked me to write a small piece about myself for inclusion in the Londoner's Diary. I wrote, among other things: 'Life in California is very beautiful, very hygienic, very tiring and very expensive.' The editor, or somebody, left out 'beautiful'.

Bingo . . . The statement with my name attached was in the *New York Times*, syndicated in newspapers from East to West, and—alas—broadcast on the Alka-Seltzer programme from San Francisco. Now at last my name was known in California. Everybody, it seemed, my mother-in-law, the local priest, the owner of the bookshop, the man at the liquor-store, far-flung friends driving up and down the Highway with their radios switched on—all heard the Alka-Seltzer programme and my subversive remarks. I woke up one morning to find myself infamous. Letters from that side were like crushed ice.

What made this all the sadder was that 1949 had finally established me as a case of Transatlantic schizophrenia. America was in my bloodstream. I had become a cat and a dog in one. Enchanted as I was to be back in England, I knew most happily that I now belonged to both sides. Still in this daze of myopic content I began to note my impressions of my home-coming. (I had been away more than a year.) Presently I put these into an article and the *Standard* published it under the title 'A Bewildered Look at England'. It was an affectionate, light-hearted piece and it raised all hell. The correspondence accused me variously. To some I was a Communist; to others a Fascist; to all a traitor, who had transferred my allegiance from my homeland, who came strutting back, loaded with dollars, to be rude. Umbrage was taken particularly at my quoting a chemist who had said 'What we want is a dictator' in the matter of some bath-salts I was trying to buy. Some people thought I meant *I* wanted a dictator; others thought I shouldn't use or expect bath-salts, and a chemist, after setting out the bath-salt situation (it still remained obscure) begged me to try to be loyal to the country of my passport. It was all very distressing, except to the features-editor who was delighted, and decided to employ me as regularly as he could.

It was also confusing. I had thought America to be the place where umbrage grew wild. I had, I believed, made a discovery about Nanny Integrity in this regard. I had expounded it, saying that Nanny couldn't really flourish so long as I lived in U.S.A. Because, I said, living out of one's own country was like being in somebody else's house and having to be polite all the time. Drawn on by one lively listener, I added that I never felt like this in France. Was it the language or what?

'You know what it is. It's because we all want to be loved,' said my listener: 'The great American need. We must be loved. Stop being polite for once. Don't you agree?'

'Yes, I think I do.'

'Well, stick with it. That's the way we are. Don't you lose your mind saying, "Yes, it's wonderful" when we all tell you how gorgeous it is to live in California? You know perfectly well we'd cut your throat—or our own—if you didn't say Yes . . . Don't we get in your hair when we sob about Europeans loving us not for ourselves but for our dollars?'

She was a wit and a poet, and she brought out the worst in me on that occasion. She quoted a Highway-side advertisement, reading 'BE POPULAR! LEARN TO PLAY A MUSICAL INSTRUMENT.' The two of us, hated by all, went to town with the American need to be loved by all.

Now, in '49, pondering the letters from those who had read the *Standard* article (as a change from the letters about the Alka-Seltzer programme) I asked myself whether the English also wanted to be loved. I had said often that we didn't give a damn what anyone thought of us. Was I wrong? Was this a belated discovery born of my new half-cat, half-dog transformation?

I decided it wasn't: and have seen no reason to change the decision since. English umbrage is of a tougher, less plaintively persistent sort than American. It isn't a matter of our wanting to be loved; it is a matter of our knowing there's nothing wrong with us and that criticism is therefore unwarranted. I am perplexed because, although we can nowadays call a spade a bloody shovel in print, although the popular press goes its startling way unchallenged, we cannot express opinions with equal freedom. Never, surely, were so many offended so easily by so little. Never surely was the fear of giving offence to this or that nation, to this or that creed, to this or that body of opinion, so big a bogey. Stately, pained rebukes, crawling apologies and wholesale withdrawals tumble over one another. In England, I would say, umbrage appears to be taken thrice daily after meals.

Americans have more of a racial-and-religious-umbrage-problem than we do. Particularly on the radio, where the word 'Jew' has to be left out of *The Merchant of Venice*, which makes the play sound very odd from time to time. If you have cause to mention a Jew on the air, you must be careful to call him a 'gentleman of the Jewish faith'. I did on one occasion point out that it would be correct to describe me as a half-Jewish lady of the Catholic Faith, but the observation was thought to be in bad taste. I told the chairman, during another radio session, that I took part in religious discussions on the B.B.C. He blinked. I said they were a lot of fun. At my description of my friend

Marghanita Laski witnessing for atheism and me witnessing for Christianity, he drank some water.

I came up against a piece of American Advertiser's umbrage while correcting the proofs of my last novel. I had mentioned a thermos flask. The copy-editor attached a note to the galley, recommending a change here. The American Thermos company insists that every time a Thermos product is mentioned it is precisely identified. In this case I should have to put 'Thermos vacuum-bottle'. Which, as the copy-editor accurately assumed, I might not want to do. I suppressed the immediate temptation to revise the sentence so that it read 'the leaky, unreliable Th-rm-s vacuum-bottle with the ill-fitting stopper.' But I became fascinated. I still am. I've always thought of a Thermos as being just a Thermos: i.e. a flask or jug that keeps hot things hot and cold things cold. Well, the flask now appears to be a vacuum-bottle; the jug is, I presume, a vacuum-jug. But is that all? What are the other sorts of Thermi, Thermice, Thermoses . . . got it, Thermoi? And what the devil is an American manufacturer doing dictating the words in a novel anyway?

2

One aspect of my Transatlantic schizophrenia is the way an idea can change its nationality overnight. If the first dazzling blink of it comes to me in the United States, the chances are that characters and background will look American. If I return to England while it is still no more than a beguiling ghost, the chances are that it will, somewhere between Idlewild and Hampstead, begin to take on

English clothing. Sometimes it suffers a sea-change on the Cunard Line. And sometimes it does more than that.

Two writers from New York have recently published their crossings-out; recording every drop of blood and sweat spilled as their creative works proceeded. Both books add up to 'what hell it all is when it goes wrong and how spiffing when the finished product turns out to be a hit.' There needs no ghost, my Lord . . . it always is.

To publish my own crossings-out is not my habit. But something like it must happen here. I must, I see, go into more than usually subjective detail if I am to illustrate the hazards of toting an idea to and fro across the Atlantic: and then tell the sequel. Here we go.

I'm no dramatist, but sometimes the idea as it begins to haunt me looks like a play. This one did. The time was March 1958 and the place was Philadelphia. I was back-stage in the Locust Street Theatre, talking to Tyrone Power; while we talked I was studying the beauty of his face, as I had studied it before, and suddenly there was a message in my head; four words only: *A man who escapes*. The message flashed and was gone. But I knew it, I thought, for the authentic sound upon the air. Once again something had stirred, come alive, appointed a rendezvous.

Nothing to do about it, as usual, but wait. Back in New York the precarious flutter-winged clue survived; the first of the mist began to clear and the blurred figures to walk in. Glancing occasionally over my shoulder, I saw them come. First the man, who looked like Tyrone and brought his name with him, the name of Daniel. Then the woman from whom he escaped and the girl with whom he ran away. The ragged outlines of their story did not however look like a novel at all. This was, surely, a play in its early stages.

'I believe,' I said to Tyrone a little later, 'that I'm in labour with a play for you.' I wondered if this were just a brag, but the play form held throughout the ensuing weeks wherein the idea lit up, dimmed down, vanished and returned according to its perplexing habit. There was a kind of theme-song to it; there often is; a talisman-phrase that keeps the first vibration alive. This time it was 'Off with the raggle-taggle gypsies O.' When nothing much seemed to be happening to these people, the theme-song could convince me that they were alive behind the mist, that the mist would presently clear and let them come close again.

But—a play? All my efforts in the theatre had been failures so far. I tried not to think about that. When I flew back to England the beguiling ghost was still with me, but a week of London and the Book Society saw it imperilled. 'It had better be a play' I thought grimly; novels were beginning to frighten me. Up to forty books a month would come in for reading. I was kept busy opening the door to large brown-paper packages. I was kept even busier rushing to the sorting-office in pursuit of those packages which had failed to find me at home and left their reproachful signals on the mat. The dining-room (it is also my study) began to diminish in floor-space as I stacked the bound proofs all around the walls. Two months of reading and reviewing almost exorcised the raggle-taggle gypsies.

Then I set out for France, for the last of five summers at La Colle-sur-Loup. The small stone house above the valley was to be given up. (No more of the sunlight on the terrace, no more of the shadow walking up the hill at evening to the Roman profile of St Paul-de-Vence against the sky.) It had been the perfect place for work and play. We drove down through the Dordogne in a mood of half-mourning, to find it again and to lose it for always.

172

Once we got there, my private magic moved in over-night. Despite the continuing Book Society parcels (*'Encore un colis pour vous, Madame, cent-cinquante à payer'*) despite the continued reading and reviewing, my friend Daniel grew in stature. He was an American with a State Department job and his wife was an ace dress-designer, a band-wagon bitch who operated in New York. Daniel, before the play's opening, had escaped from her. Deliberately he had taken flight while still under the clouds of a McCarthy investigation. He was innocent but nothing on earth would make him stay and prove it. Content in the knowledge that so long as he remained suspect, his beastly wife would be glad to let him go, he contrived to vanish. He had been living for five years as a hermit beside the village of La Colle. I gave him our house.

Here he met the girl (who had taken on British nationality since my acquaintance with her in New York.) Here, to his horror, he learned that his innocence was established. The nasty little man, Horace Figg, who turned informer, like Budenz, when the witch-hunt was at its height, had now assumed white garments of repentance, and told the truth. From Figg, Daniel learned that the world and the band-wagon wife were out to reinstate him; the wife was already on his track. Only one escape-route remained to him: a fake death.

I worked on this plan while our last weeks at La Colle ran out. We were besieged from dawn to dusk by people who wanted—or did not want—to buy the furniture. It went on and on. I remember two *antiquaires*, arch-disparagers, who arrived before breakfast. Nothing in the house was of the slightest interest (*'C'est très rustique, vous savez'*) except a picture that was not for sale. A female *antiquaire* drove up while we were out and removed from the terrace the two earthenware pots she had declined the day before. Strangers came ducking in through the door in the wall at odd hours. (*'Je m'interesse au guéridon, Madame'; 'Permettez voir le frigidaire?'*) We staggered across the terrace, helping carry heavy chairs and tables to be lashed to the backs of decrepit cars. Wads of filthy mille-franc notes flew about. A rhythmic battle developed with the *voisins* who wanted the beds at once instead of waiting till we'd finished sleeping in them. Gradually the furniture, lamps and carpets disappeared. It was all very sad and tiring and rather like *The Cherry Orchard*. But Daniel and the play somehow throve on it.

I saw this stripping of the house as the opening of Act Three, after the fake death. The terrace itself and the two front rooms had formed themselves into a manageable set. Now it was time to make notes; they were made before we left La Colle and drove sorrowfully northward. All was in order.

There were two outstanding snags. The first I knew how to tackle . . . or thought I did. If Daniel was a State Department official under investigation, he couldn't leave America on his own passport. I would have to give him dual nationality and show somewhere that he had used his British passport for the escape. Not that this process would come within the action of the play itself, but I would stay fussed, I thought, until I got some expert advice on the procedure and knew exactly what had happened.

The second snag was more ominous. I didn't really feel at home with a play. I had it all lined up, but I found I was looking at the characters from the front, in that fatal, cardboard, exit-and-entrance perspective of paralysis which affects me as soon as I move over into the dramatic field. I wasn't inside their heads. I was outside, watching them from the stalls.

This wouldn't do. Nor would my reluctance to sit down to it once we were in London. But when Tyrone Power arrived, on his way to Spain, my courage came back. I could, I discovered, tell him the bare bones of the play without feeling shy. As he left our house after lunch he said he would like to do it in England next autumn. But my courage sank down when he had gone. At the end of two days' brooding, the solution came. In a sudden dazzle of peace I saw that I could write this first as a story. That was the way to be free and have no more fears. In a story of fifteen thousand words I could roam at ease as usual. After that, when I had got to know them all on paper, I could put the story into dramatic form. Shouting *Deo gratias* I began to map it out.

In October, I sailed for New York, something of a fugitive from the Book Society. With me went the minimum of page-proofs to read. With me also went Daniel; his wife; her best friend; a French curé; the ghost of the La Colle house; Horace Figg; various minor characters; and of course the girl who at this stage had lost her name as well as her face but made her entrance on a runaway motor-bike. With me, best of all, went the title; it had turned up earlier than I expected. It enclosed the story perfectly. It was 'Can't Catch Me'.

Normally I have such trouble dredging for titles that this seemed a good omen. I was heartened also by a last-minute message from Tyrone in Spain. He hoped, the letter said, that my baby was alive and kicking, like his own: the child who was to be born in the spring.

I recognised, as I boarded the ship, an untrustworthy state of euphoria. My reason for going to New York was the publication of a novel there. It was the first (and I hope the last) time I ever persuaded myself that the journey itself would be an investment. I saw, stretching ahead, eight weeks wherein I would indulge publicity-capers for the sake of the book and spend all the rest of my waking hours writing 'Can't Catch Me'. I had money in my purse; not enough to excuse the trip, but enough to make it possible. My mood was my gambler's mood when I enter the Casino. All the chances looked favourable.

On the journey I was prevented from beginning the story because of a longish review that had to be shot swiftly back to the Book Society. The month's Choice was my beloved John Marquand's *Women and Thomas Harrow*. When I had got the review typed in the purser's office, I saw no more barriers between me and the work to be done. Except, of course, that trifling matter of Daniel's passport. Any good New York lawyer could surely put me right about those legalities.

Now the skyline again; and now the lure that New York likes to dangle at the beginning: a glitter, a promise, a suggestion of Tom Tiddler's Ground. A photographer looming up on the dockside posed me sitting on somebody else's luggage. He had plenty of time. The customs-examination saw to that. An iris bulb, which I had been asked to give to Eva Le Gallienne, was taken away and X-rayed. A roll of Shetland tweed, which I had been asked to give to Merle Oberon, was diagnosed as an import, removed and assessed for duty. The mink coat which I had been asked to hand to Leueen MacGrath (whose property it was) kept me warm while the minutes strung out into hours. I was pleased with my publisher for having sent the photographer along until I discovered that he was the regular photographer for the Cunard Line.

The first days did nothing to damage 'Can't Catch Me'. On the contrary. I stayed aloft in my apartment at the Wellington Hotel, beguiled by the view, dodging my book's notices in the press, planning the publicity-capers and bringing the story to the boil. I set enquiries about the passport-situation going; and that was how I received a telephone-call from Mrs Harriet Pilpel who was not only a lawyer but utterly charming and deeply interested. In the course of putting my problem to her I made the story sound a little more like the Alger Hiss case than it was. Could a man in those circumstances get away before the investigation began, provided that he owned an up-to-date British passport? Mrs Pilpel was all set to discover. Our talk sent me off on another journey in my own head. Should the story (though not the play) begin, after all, in New York and Washington 1952? I had long wanted to take a crack at the McCarthy horror . . . And the ambiance of New York made me see, most clearly, an American beginning: the prelude to it all, Daniel making his escape. This gave a chance of meeting the wife, the dress-designer, on her home ground. I promptly harried my cousin, Ethel Frankau of Bergdorf Goodman, for some authentic low-down on designers.

When the letter arrived from Mrs Pilpel's office, I saw that I had somehow slanted my question wrongly. The letter told me much, but not the thing I needed to know. I telephoned her to put the problem tidy and apologised for causing her trouble. Not a bit: she would do further research and we would meet when I returned from a flying visit to the South.

There came a golden day, the best kind of New York weather. I walked alone, slightly drunk with the air and the sunshine; two people had called up to say that Orville

Prescott of the *Times* had written a rave review of my novel. I wouldn't let them read it to me, but it was nice to know it was there. As usual, Nanny conducted a hectoring argument with me about this: 'If you don't read them why should you care if they're good or bad?'

'Score to you' I said. 'Never mind.' But Nanny always minds.

I was just loping in the direction of a drugstore when the fabric of 'Can't Catch Me' began to deepen and solidify in my head. Perhaps I had turned to it in an effort to dodge Nanny. I don't remember; I only know that it suddenly took on new life, new colour: it spread itself out before my eyes, beautiful and whole and clamouring to be written.

I went past the drugstore, on down East 54th to the Chateaubriand, my favourite New York restaurant. Here I treated myself to an elegant, expensive lunch. Daniel and the rest stood around the table. I sat on, leaning my cheek against all of it. The dream kept me still.

I saw the opening scene: New York, with the bitch-wife in a temperamental tantrum; Daniel downtown meeting Horace Figg, the informer, in all innocence, thinking he needed help. I saw Daniel return to find the tantrum raging. I saw the telegram arrive, summoning him to attend the McCarthy investigation. Now he was slipping gently away from trouble, the telegram in his pocket. Now he was at the air-terminal (Mrs Pilpel had better fix that passport: this scene could be good) and now he was free. Now France, five years after. All went smoothly, vividly past my eyes as I smoked and drank more coffee and let it run to its end.

The exhilaration stayed with me, through the afternoon to the evening. There was a dinner-party at my publisher's house. (J. B. Priestley greeted my entrance by saying in heavy aside to his neighbour, 'I happen to know she's been writing in the *New York Times* for years under the name of Orville Prescott.') I was light-headed, and foolish enough to talk of 'Can't Catch Me'. It was, I said a story that would, in texture and atmosphere, be rather like 'The Duchess and the Smugs'. I honestly thought so, too. The moon and the fantasy-ending on the terrace at La Colle made me think so. I said, and believed, that I was all set to begin it in two days time, when I went south.

'Wonderful. Did Mrs Pilpel solve the passport problem for you?'

'She's working on it,' I said. 'No hurry.'

'It couldn't be a novel, this one?'

'No; not enough there. When it's done, I'm turning it into a play for Tyrone Power.' I talked too much, about everything, that night.

When I flew South I left the Book Society proofs behind, and took only my notes and the clean foolscap; the launching-site. In the aeroplane I calculated that the preliminary stage had already lasted nearly eight months. Certainly it was time to be launching.

We had hired a car and driven ourselves into the dark, along the Blue Ridge Parkway, getting lost as night came; finding at last a motel in a small town. We were very late. There was just time to swallow a quick drink, get out of the motel and eat before the only restaurant shut its doors.

I can see the place still, the lighted drugstore with its counter and tables at the back. We gave our order. I caught sight of some local newspapers in a rack near the door. Since we had seen no paper that day I decided to treat us to two copies of the *Asheville Courier*.

I carried them back to the table, handing one to my

companion as I sat down. I became aware of her stillness
before I read the words on the front page of the *Asheville
Courier*. The words were 'Tyrone Power dies in Spain.'

3

I came back to New York with the foolscap as clean as ever
and the notes untouched. I found a letter from one of the
Harper's Magazine editors asking if he could have a pre-
view of the new story that was to be like 'The Duchess and
the Smugs.' I found much data from Mrs Pilpel and she
came up to my hotel, looking as elegant as Harlequin, to
have a drink and discuss the passport-problem, which was
proving a little craggy. Inside I felt sure that the springs
of this story had finally broken, that I wouldn't now be
able to write it. But I tried to keep it alive by whistling in
the dark, talking about it a great deal and protesting that
Tyrone's death made it all the more important to get the
work, that had begun with him, finished in his honour.

I was deflected to book-reviews on the voyage home. I
wasn't sorry to leave New York. It had been a ruinous,
doom-ridden trip in all sorts of ways. Among other dooms,
my novel had flopped; my publicity-capers had gone for
nothing; I had spent far too much money and done no work
worth mentioning.

And here came Christmas. At New Year the Book Society parcels seemed to arrive every hour on the hour.
Another letter from Mrs Pilpel established the passport-
situation and then I got the bill for the research. Halfway
through January I pulled myself together and sat down
at my desk, with all the notes, to try and build again. Surely
a story that had lived with me almost a year couldn't die,

even though Tyrone was dead and all my excitement over
. . . I would not admit defeat. I would bring these people
to life again.

The regular hours at the desk produced only a routine
of writing long letters to myself. In the letters the story
turned back into a play, then switched to a story again.
La Colle turned into the Dordogne. The wife turned into
a French châtelaine. Horace Figg turned into twin broth-
ers. The American background faded. Daniel became an
Irishman, which solved the passport problem but seemed
kind of mean to Mrs Pilpel. The fake death looked silly
and I scrapped it altogether, leaving myself without an
end. The girl, who had, I saw, been thoroughly tiresome all
through, was now completely invisible.

Gradually, as I scribbled and searched, the colour de-
parted; the life went. There was nothing here any more
except the dark, laughing face of a man who escaped . . .
and a flicker of light still playing over the line 'Off with
the raggle-taggle gypsies O.'

So I was back in the desert of the time before the idea
comes. But this was worse than usual; an idea had come
and gone, leaving a whole wasted year behind it.

4

So much for the journeyings.

Despite the cold-blowing airs of my financial situation
there was, I decided, no hope for any idea so long as I
stayed with the Book Society. I resigned in March and the
airs blew colder still. I prowled restlessly for three weeks
before I glanced over my shoulder, and saw Daniel again.
He was Daniel with a difference; still with the defiant

'Can't Catch Me' for his slogan, still with the raggle-taggle gypsies for his song. These, with the dark, laughing look, were the only survivals from his earlier equipment. He confounded me further by seeming to be a boy of nineteen.

I brooded. His escape, I observed, was as unlike the first escape as could be imagined. It was a flight from his world into loss of memory. But was this to be a play—or a story? Neither. It was a novel.

As the other characters moved in behind him I didn't recognise a soul. The original cast had vanished. The new cast seemed lively and willing, particularly—surprise, surprise—the girl, who arrived on the scene in one vivid flash. She startled me by being fat, but she had a beautiful face. I called her Antonia.

Well, all right: good enough: a book.

The first step was to take medical advice on amnesia. (This was a few months before the Podola case made every aspect of it available to a wide public.) I sat with my long list of questions, badgering a doctor and a psychiatrist who remained courteous and helpful. Their one ruling—that loss of memory was usually the refuge of the simple mind—didn't worry me. Daniel, even in his first reincarnation, had never been a complex or over-sensitive person. His simplicity suited his fate.

I discarded 'Can't Catch Me' for 'Case-History of Daniel Black.' He was the child of divorce and the first chapters of the Rough became a prologue wherein the four people concerned, father and current wife, mother and current husband, gave accounts of themselves and the situation from which the boy had run. He would, I thought, run to Ireland: live magically free of his past, fall in love with God and the girl. The return of memory I saw as tragedy for him, the cold truth breaking the dream and the fairy-tale. But magic would win; it couldn't not.

There were, as ever, a number of hurdles. I didn't quite see how the disappearance of a boy of nineteen could last three months—as I planned—without conspiracy. And I knew nothing of Ireland (except the territory which a policeman, to whom we later gave a lift in Castlebar, called The Occupied Counties.) Cautiously I tried Daniel out in France. It didn't work. America? Impossible.

I had finished the prologue, nearly a hundred pages, when we set out in May. I had not travelled deliberately in search of a background since I went mountain-hunting in Switzerland nearly thirty years before. It was wonderfully good fun. We drove south, to Cashel and Bantry Bay; west, to Connemara. I was already in love with Ireland when we got to Adare, County Limerick. I took two days exploring the village and the demesne in a heavy downpour. This was it. But I wanted another sort of house in the demesne, not a great house, merely a mournful ex-mansion in a bad way. The church in Adare wasn't right either. I collected the right church at Cong. Reaching Dundalk I found a house that looked as if it would do.

We spent the night of June the Twelfth at Dundalk. There was a continued magic upon the journey: one of the things I discovered in Ireland was that I consistently dreamed forward and even thought forward while still awake, seeing ahead in time. (I still do that when I am there.) Anyone who shares my devotion to St Anthony will understand why I like June the Thirteenth. It was on this morning that I heard a whisper in my mind.

'Daniel doesn't only lose his memory. He picks up his father's memory as soon as he gets to the village' the whisper said: 'He goes on where his father left off, thirty years ago.'

I stood contemplating a large bowl of pinks, whose scent was delicate, yet strong. Moted sunshine hung through the window into a wide, cool corridor that felt haunted. I was pleased.

The 1959 summer put a sun-tan on the faces of all Londoners except me. I spent the summer in the dining-room with Daniel. Something of the Ireland magic had persuaded me that this would, at last, prove an easy book to write.

By September I knew it for the hardest job I ever tackled. The 'click' was so long in coming that I can't now remember being conscious of it at any time. Fairytale? It was bewitched, bedevilled, demon-haunted. The characters behaved themselves pretty well when the story let them. It was the actual story that developed a kind of St Vitus's dance, refusing to stay still or submit to a shape. It played an air-balloon trick, a will o' the wisp trick, in fact a 'Can't Catch Me' trick. The prologue danced into the middle, changing as it went. The three-months span shrank down to three weeks. A maddening Irish policeman got in and was liquidated only with the utmost difficulty. Every time I reached what I thought was a peak of the action, a dénouement, it suddenly wasn't there. This was largely caused by Daniel's flat refusal to reveal to anyone the fact that he had lost his memory. He went on keeping it a secret and I gave up trying to force him. By October I had four overlapping versions of the Rough and still only two-thirds of the story on paper.

Sternly I decided to have done with this nonsense and start on the Smooth right away. I put the prologue back at the beginning and changed the title to *The Heir*. Finding my way through the various versions, wire-puzzle work among hundreds of besottedly-scrawled pages, was the worst of it. No, not quite. The worst was the knowledge that the three-weeks span must now boil down to three days. The fantasy wouldn't stand up to three weeks.

We seemed to be moving at last. But I was well behind schedule when I came to Ireland again to check details with the Trinity College Librarian and revisit Adare. I made this wintry journey alone; writing in the train, writing in the Dunraven Arms while the short afternoon light faded off the trees of the demesne across the road.

I was by now down to the bottom of my bank-account. 'And just as far as ever from the end.' Well, not quite. Ireland had helped. At which point somebody told me that Victoria Sackville-West had written a novel called *The Heir*. Of course she had. I had read it . . . Silly of me.

On the Twenty-sixth of November I battled my way through to the end of what, for all its intended smoothness, was two-thirds Rough. I put paid to the last chapter in my father's study down at Hove, a blessèd place for work if there ever was one. I felt like Edmund Hillary shouting 'Done the old bitch!' as he came down from Everest. The title, by the way, was now *The Prunus Tree*. (Certainly we had had trees—Apple, Nutmeg, Jacaranda and the one that grew in Brooklyn. Never mind; this was quite pretty.)

The Prunus Tree, though by that time I seemed to have been writing it for ten years, was not much more than seventy thousand words long. I got the Smooth done by January and had just given it to the typist when it occurred to me that the true title was *Road Through The Woods*. The typist had just finished typing the prologue when it occurred to me that the prologue ought to go in the middle after all; which played hell with the page-numbering.

By now I had lost my nerve and would awake dreading a further revelation about this plague of a book. I didn't dare throw away the Rough, or the voluminous notes. Nothing more developed, however, until the day my publisher telephoned to say he liked it. This brought on a period of peace, followed by the realisation, as I cooked the dinner, that somewhere in the first half I had left out two paragraphs of vital importance. All the typescripts were halted in their tracks. I inserted the revised pages at the publisher's office and we had a cup of tea.

Next day the dining-room seemed very quiet and empty, the way it always does after the end. Now there was really and truly nothing left to do but jettison the Rough and destroy the notebooks. Still, it took me a couple of hours to remove all traces of *Can't Catch Me, Case-History of Daniel Black, The Heir, The Prunus Tree* and *Road Through The Woods*. With them went a whole sheaf of correspondence from the American lawyer's office concerning Daniel's immigration-status, and a fleeting conviction that the title, after all, should be *Mrs Pilpel's Passport*.

CHAPTER
NINE

1

'Are you—a Roman Catholic?'

The young woman had, as my punctuation indicates, paused halfway. After the pause she had lowered her voice and spoken hurriedly. (The inflexion reminded me of far-off elderly aunts asking, 'Do you want to go to—the lavatory?') This interview, for a local paper, had proceeded gaily until now.

Not any more. She was avoiding my eye, gazing downward, riffling the pages of her shorthand book. Embarrassment about religion being a fairly common English symptom, I said 'Yes', and hoped I'd put her out of her misery, so we could go on to the next thing.

Still avoiding my eye, she snapped 'That's what my mother thought. I gave her your book to read. She said it was Roman Catholic Propaganda.' There was a little note of triumph sounding: Bully For Mum.

I found myself agreeing in part that it was Bully For Mum. The book was *The Bridge,* my tale of transit through Purgatory. Mum, unlike some readers, had at least caught on to the fact of Purgatory. And I knew something else about Mum now. She wasn't sympathetic to my Church.

187

Had she been in any way drawn to it, she would not have said Propaganda.

Propaganda, when one applied the word to fiction, meant sales-talk for a product one wouldn't dream of buying. Didn't it? I searched my mind, trying to remember if anyone had ever said of a novel, 'And what's more, it's jolly good propaganda.' I could recall no single instance of this. Meanwhile I was keeping the young woman waiting.

She was no longer embarrassed. She looked me coolly in the eye, waiting for me to confirm or dispute her mother's diagnosis.

I explained, as best I could, that Catholicism was a part of me, a part of my nature; that this must show in my work, along with some other natural interests, like France and America, like the truth, like gambling.

'No,' she said, 'those aren't the same. Because you're a Catholic, you're a *committed* writer.'

'Is that a handicap, in your view?'

'It must be, mustn't it?'

'Why?'

'Well, you've told me your duty is to the work itself—to nothing else.' She flicked a page of the shorthand book, rereading her notes. 'Here. You said it was just between you and old Nanny Integrity.'

'So what's your worry?'

She frowned. I realized that my close friends might accuse me of being 'sunny', which according to them means being snide, with a surface pseudo-sweetness of manner covering my determination to meet nobody halfway. (*'Promise* not to be sunny tonight . . .' a plaintive voice echoed in memory.) I was ashamed. This young woman was serious and I knew perfectly well what her worry was.

188

She was thinking of rockets from the Bishop, warnings from the Vatican to toe the party line; she saw me beset by restrictions and refusing to admit they were there.

How to assure her that Nanny had never taken a beating since my conversion? As to *The Bridge*, I wanted, I said, to write a book about Purgatory because I believed in Purgatory, because the thought of Purgatory interested me. Was my central character conceived in propagandist mood? A man baptized a Catholic, scarcely aware of it, going through life without any true consciousness or knowledge of his Faith. A believer in God, yes. But a fubsy kind of believer, with a tremendous sympathy for all churches and all creeds. 'Do you,' I asked, 'find David Neilson a really resounding advertisement for Rome?'

'You made him get to Heaven.'

'Well yes; that was the object of the exercise.'

'Would you have made it happen if he hadn't been a Roman Catholic?'

I said 'That character was the way he was, if you follow me: which means I can't see him any other way. But if he'd come to me differently, he might still have got to Heaven. After all, he wasn't the only one to get there, was he? What about his wife?'

Here she said with a touch of severity, 'The wife who committed suicide . . . Yes. Was that because David had baptized her?'

'It was.'

'Could that make it all right?'

'We're running into technicalities,' I warned her.

'Don't you think it's rather foxing for your readers to be presented with things they don't understand?'

I thought about it. 'In one way, yes. In another, no. If the reader found the whole issue obscure and the scene completely meaningless, then yes. But that would be because I hadn't written it well enough. If I want to write of a specifically Catholic matter, I'm in much the same position as when I want to write about anything else. I must be as clear on paper as I am in my head. Take the baptism. You knew, as a reader, that Linda wanted it. You saw it happen to her. The glimpse of Heaven came in the very last lines of the book. There you saw the result. Even if you couldn't believe it, you weren't totally foxed. You haven't asked me "What did all that mean?" You've said "Was it because David baptized her?" So I've *suggested* a meaning to you. And that's what I'd hope to do when I write from the Catholic angle. The non-Catholic can't fully share the world of my experience; so he can't use exactly the same lens I'm using to look at it. But I ought to be able to give him a picture as it's a world I happen to know from inside. The same might go for the roulette table—if he'd never played roulette.'

'Yes, but. . .'

'What's the "but"?'

'We've got away from being committed. Making a scene clear isn't the same thing. Perhaps I didn't put the question right. What I want to know is this: Hasn't being a Catholic ever stopped you from saying something you *really* wanted to say?'

'Not in my recollection. And isn't the sign of a committed writer, almost, you might call it, the case against him, that he's *got* something he really wants to say?'

She agreed, reluctantly.

'I don't think you mean to question my sincerity as a Catholic,' I told her, 'but you're getting rather near it, are you not?'

'How?'

'Well, you began by suggesting, via your mother, that what I wrote was propaganda. Now you imply that I can't write what I really want to say. Put those two together and what do we get?'

'I'm sorry.' She made a note. 'Will you let me describe you as an *unconscious* salesman—or saleswoman—for Roman Catholicism?'

'If you like.'

'And would you agree that all Catholic writers are just that?'

'Maybe. Certainly it's an occupational risk.'

'You don't—you never have consciously tried to sell your beliefs?'

My immediate reaction was that I, the guinea-pig for experiment, had never been primarily concerned with selling anything, not even my books.

Then I remembered Cambridge, Massachusetts, the kitchen table where I sat down, as told in Chapter Three, to write the first novel after the wartime gap. It was also my first novel as a Catholic. The year was 1946. I had been received into the Church in 1942.

2

Certainly there was a new element on the air. I had seen it coming, weeks before the first, flutter-winged clue. This way:

I was reading an American novel, by a writer I admired. It was good, I thought, as I raced through the opening chapters. A man-and-woman, love-and-marriage story. Adult, lively, sensual. At first, I found it hard to put the book down. After a while I found some difficulty in picking it up. I asked myself why. What was it this novel lacked? Never before, with the author's work, had I felt my interest blowing away. I couldn't take these people seriously. For all their glitter, they seemed immature, half-fledged. They were just beginning to bore me stiff when I found the reason. There was no hint of God anywhere in the book. Not even a denial of God. For the writer, as for his characters, God just didn't come up.

I was disconcerted; not by the book, by my own reaction. Surely I myself had in the past written such novels— plenty of them. I hadn't one to hand. I could, of course, hunt some down in the stacks at Widener Library. But that wasn't really necessary. I could remember well enough that in my cruising days, my time of uncertainty, I had often written without giving God a thought or a place on the page.

What, I asked myself, was going to happen next? Had I turned, without realising it, into a Hot-Gospeller for Rome? Were all my books, from here on out, to be religious in theme and flavour? It was a teasing question. It went with me while I walked over Boston Common, or paced beside the Charles River, awaiting the old, lost stir upon the quiet, the long-delayed hint of rendezvous. I was free at last to write again. All I needed was for the clue to come.

It came; and, as I have said, the new element came with it. Useless to fight. I could no more see these people without their spiritual lives than I could see them without their heads.

I was over-excited. I had got hold of something new. I was also, from time to time, uneasy and self-conscious. Against all my vows I was aware of a world outside the study—I mean kitchen—door. This uneasiness came not from the fear of angering a Bishop, shocking the Ladies' Sodality, or getting across the Vatican. The world outside was the world of expert Catholics waiting, possibly, to catch me on a technical error. Part of the self-consciousness arose from a dread of making the whole issue sound easy and smug. At other times I let my convert's exuberance have its head. This, as I recall, was the only true joy in that whole laborious struggle to relearn my former trade. My sole pleasure consisted in waving the Papal flag.

Looking at *Shaken in the Wind* nowadays, I recognise the sort of book to be expected from the new convert. The Catholics have all the fun as well as all the answers. It isn't altogether a bad novel (the 'easiness with the words', I'll remind you, helped it), but it shouts its creed from the house-tops. It makes a loud, overt statement of my belief.

Yes, then, to my young interviewer. I was consciously selling my Faith at that time.

Did I succeed?

That's something else again . . . I remember most clearly a bitter reproach from an agnostic friend. She wrote pages. She rebuked me for my all-out attack on Catholicism. She assumed, she said, that I had 'lapsed'. Even so— and admitting her own dislike of the Church—she asked me how I could possibly turn and rend my former allegiance? Didn't it come under the heading of bite-the-hand-that fed me? I was too much embarrassed to reply.

Hers was the biggest misconception I remember. But quite a lot of friends thought the novel was a record of my own difficulties and discouragements when *en route* for my conversion. It wasn't. The difficulties and discouragements were, however, much more palpable to them than anything else.

Why?

I remember the reaction to Evelyn Waugh's *Brideshead Revisited:* people asking me anxiously whether he would be excommunicated; whether I, as a Catholic, approved of a story in which sinful, beastly Catholics predominated? (And I have had many a similar heckling about Graham Greene.)

The answer, I think, is obvious. A part of it lies in what I said to the young woman. The Catholic writes of the world of his own experience; since it isn't a universal experience, not even the most sympathetic outsider knows it as the writer knows it. Nor, I believe, would he expect to, were the problems other than religious problems. Reading a novel about engineering, for example, he wouldn't question the technicalities unless he was an engineer. But religion looks deceptively easy to understand. Agnostics and humanists feel no inhibitions when discussing it. They aren't afraid of getting hold of the wrong end of the stick.

The state of mind in which I wrote *Shaken in the Wind* is now long ago and far away. Nineteen years of Catholicism have brought a different temper. Still it remains impossible, as I said to the interviewer, to hide altogether the part of my nature that is my belief.

At its simplest: I see people as human beings with souls. But some of my characters may not be aware of their souls at all. Then I must, for full understanding, for honest presentation, live under their skins, be the Godless as well as the believer.

Is this hard for me? Not in the least. No harder than to live under the skin of an elderly Italian princess, of a doctor, of a schoolboy . . . What would be hard would be to write a book like the American novel I mentioned, a book in which there was no hint of God anywhere. Yet I never plan for Him; He just shows up.

It would be affected for me to strive to keep Him out; to write determinedly as though He didn't exist. I should be keeping myself in artificial chains. I should be performing a kind of acrobatic all the time. Can I find an analogy to make this clearer?

Well, let us suppose I'm writing a book about a blind man. I should make every effort to 'be' him, to experience in my imagination what blindness means. But somewhere along the line you would get a hint that I can see. Why not? It wouldn't be a part of my aim to fool you, the reader, that I myself am blind.

Would I be pleased if you did, by chance, come to this conclusion? Or suppose, writing of an atheist, I could persuade you that I was this person? Wouldn't either achievement prove my skill? Well, it might. But I'm willing to swear it couldn't happen. Whether I presented you with a convincing blind man or a convincing atheist, somewhere you'd still get a clue about me.

Then I'm now safe, am I, from the kind of outside misconception that arose when my agnostic chum read *Shaken in the Wind?* Is that what I mean? Have the nineteen years entrenched me so firmly behind a Roman wall that I'm established forever as an 'unconscious salesman' for the Faith? And is this what finally solves the dilemma of the committed writer? The dilemma, that is, between his integrity as an artist and his loyalty to his commitment.

Better writers than I, deeper minds than my own, have acknowledged the dilemma and examined it. Am I merely fortunate because I haven't encountered it yet? What I told the interviewer still holds good. Being a Catholic has never stopped me from saying what I want to say.

I think I can offer a better reason than mere good fortune. Because, after all, Catholicism isn't just a matter of knowing certain things but of being a certain kind of person through and through. The inside knowledge belonging to the religious writer is only a part of his whole person. His wholeness may be compared, as I see it, with his nationality.

Does a loyal Englishman hesitate to write freely in a novel about his own countrymen? Or a loyal American? Or a loyal Frenchman? Do we see them sitting down at their desks, stiffly aware of their duties to the land that bred them? Must they, from time to time, glance nervously at the national flag for a reminder? Could any novelist feel bound to picture his people as a race of heroes; inhibited by the thought of exploring their darkness along with their light? The idea, as I see you about to observe, is ridiculous.

For the benefit of a beginner at the trade, a Catholic writer setting out, with his Faith as much a part of him as his nose, and his creative restlessness beckoning him on, I will be more explicit.

Suppose I find one Church ruling—the marriage law, for example—particularly hard to live with. I go on subscribing to it, obeying it, knowing it's there for a reason, and trying not to complain. Among my own kind I may treat myself on occasion to a good grumble. But I'm unlikely to make a habit of discussing it with non-Catholics.

Should I, then, not write about it? If this problem really haunts me, the chances are that it may work itself sooner or later into a novel. I may not plan for it. Just the same it will achieve the subtle invasion known to all of us who ply this trade. Suddenly I shall find it there. Presently I shall find it woven so securely into the fabric that there's no hope of picking it out. What now? Should I abandon the novel, pulling up on my heels, turning resolutely away from temptation?

Well, let us see what I'm up against. Am I, in Catholic idiom, afraid of causing scandal? Am I casting an uneasy eye to the thought of the Bishop reading it at breakfast—to the Ladies' Sodality raising horrified hands? Or am I looking at the non-Catholic reader who will, if he reads this, find one more proof that the Church wields a monstrous tyranny?

Back to my old credo. I oughtn't to be looking at any of them. The work itself is the target. Everybody knows the Church has some remarkably strict rules. Their logic is hardly likely to suffer from being examined by me in a work of fiction. The Church is my love and I have always written, without fear, of my loves. No. I wouldn't hesitate to explore a Catholic difficulty in a novel, should the impulse come. I'd far rather go to it alone at my desk than in an armchair with a Scotch handy and my best agnostic friend all ears.

The devoted Catholic, in my view, is safe to write whatever he pleases. What result he achieves must, of course, depend not only on his intention but on his taste and his skill.

'*What about sex?*' is now, as Barrie says, the universal shriek. I can hear it. I have heard it often since 1942. The Church's attitude to sex is, for many outside it, the heart of the matter. They can accept, wryly and with amused tolerance, things like fish on Friday. But on the notions of celibacy, chastity, and sexual sin, they're inclined to bog down.

The flesh in our time has become so much more interesting than the spirit. Nobody, I think, would dream of asking whether as a Catholic I may legitimately write of spiritual sins or excesses. Nobody, I believe, would question my freedom to explore the paths of avarice, pride, hatred, or despair. 'The flesh' itself has come to mean sex and sex only. Nobody pays much attention to gluttony or sloth; sensuous delight in luxury is almost a virtue. Heavy drinking calls for more respectful interest, since we have decided to name it Alcoholism and treat it as a social problem. But by and large, sex wins.

I have never felt guilty about writing of sex, because I'm not by nature a sex-monger. What do I mean by a sex-monger? I mean, among others, Nabokov, James Purdy, Grace Metalious and, surprisingly perhaps, James Gould Cozzens.

When *By Love Possessed* came out, somebody who was not, I think, the greatest brain of the twentieth century questioned my objections to the scene describing sexual intercourse. That scene, this person pointed out, took place in the marriage bed. Surely I as a Catholic couldn't deplore sex in the marriage bed. Indeed, as a believer in the sacramental nature of the flesh, I ought to be cheering my head off. Except, of course, he added winsomely, that these two weren't Catholics. Did that account for my disapproval?

No. I'd still disapprove if the book had got the Imprimatur. I find the mixture of fine writing and succulent throbbery distasteful; that's all. And when it comes to charting the climax of an orgasm by means of exclamation-marks —well, anybody who's read this far can guess how *that* takes me.

I can't think, offhand, of any Catholic novelist who's also a sex-monger. The heated overtones of the sex-monger's mood are not to be caught in the work of Waugh, Greene, or Mauriac; though all have written freely about sexual intercourse.

198

To my mind there's a far more avoidable fate for the Catholic writer, particularly in America. The fate of Puritanism. Puritanism has something in common with Muzak and T.V. It dulls the ear and the eye.

My acquaintance with Catholic Puritanism or—if you like—Puritan Catholicism has been largely an American affair. The preoccupation of the American priesthood and laity alike with the sexual sin comes as a shock to the visiting foreigner. I remember my first encounter with the Legion of Decency pledge, to be repeated aloud in church after the priest. The congregation droned it out with a will; promising among other unlikelihoods, as Frank Sheed has observed, to 'do all in their power' to assist the Legion's work. For years now, lonely and obstinately aware of Nanny glowering lest I succumb, I have kept silence on this occasion. The obligation to stand up and repeat the pledge once took me unawares in a very small church in South Carolina. I was in the front pew. I held to my defection; inside I had reverted to the terror of my schooldays. The priest's eye seemed to signal 'See you in my study later.'

It was in California that a Catholic refused to go on reading my novel *The Willow Cabin* because it had adultery in it. Here also a priest engaged me in angry correspondence because I said morality (by which he meant sexual morality) could not be the final criterion when judging a work of art. This depressed and bewildered me. When I resorted to Cardinal Newman's declaration that sinless literature would mean no literature, I got a brush-off. So did literature. So did the Cardinal. Loose standards, I was reminded, were known to prevail in the churches of Europe.

Then came a period of grave warnings. Had I thought

what my novels would do to corrupt the young? Would I, for example, give a child *The Willow Cabin?*

Well, no, I wouldn't. Any more than I'd give it Burgundy or a cigar. I hope its mother wouldn't either. The kiddies' reading is her responsibility rather than mine, because I don't write for children. (Meanwhile I am still bewildered that mothers all over the lot seem content to let the child feast, unchecked, at a T.V. screen.)

The question of censorship vexes me. More, perhaps, than it used to. I am, incidentally, one who believes the publication of *Lolita* and all the advance-wuffle about it to have been a mistake. It would be informative to see a statistic of the rape of schoolgirls since the book became public property. And if this seems to contradict what I said in my last paragraph, I must point out that *Lolita* is a corrupter of the adult rather than the kiddie. Yet censorship remains a difficult pill for me to swallow. Who would censor the censors? But, oh for some automatic revolt of good taste, a surge of effective anger that would sweep away the current abysmal standards; taking with it alike the 'sweater-girls' and the slugging, the naïvety and the nastiness, the noise and the visual illiteracy to be found especially in America today. There would be a Catholic crusade indeed. And, as a 'committed' person, all I do about it is pray with some regularity. The prayer is my own. It runs, 'God, give me every day the courage of my anger and the anger of my courage.'

Which brings me to the subject of passion, the quality to be found in all 'committed' people. For a writer, to my mind, the more passion the better.

Whatever his passion, he must learn, as his technique improves, the effective control of his wild horses. At the beginning they will not only drag all his secrets out of him but appear at times to be trampling him underfoot. No matter. Restraint, control, detachment—those qualities beloved of reviewers—will come. But it would be a pity were these lessons to quench altogether the fire inside. Entirely dispassionate writers make dull reading. As Roy Campbell said, 'They use the curb and snaffle . . . but where's the bloody horse?'

The passionate Catholic, like the passionate Freudian or the passionate politician may not, at first glance, be seen for what he is because his passion directs itself to something that has its own book of rules. Must passion necessarily flout all books of rules? What about a passion for falconry, as demonstrated by T. H. White in *The Goshawk*? This might seem a strange devotion for a modern man. Yet the writer communicates his own thrill. And falconry, surely, has rules?

But they are not rules for living; they do not involve a total concept nor a crusade.

Let's move over for a moment from faith to Freud.

Suppose that psychiatry were, in my belief, the whole answer to the problem of human existence. Then it would become my faith. I should be accepting a dogma as definite, in its different way, as the dogma I accept now. I would have undergone analysis. My total concept, my view of mankind, would be established. I would see a pattern, a design. I would know that the flaws in this pattern are made in earliest childhood, and I would recognise the remedy. Looking at humanity through this precise, particular lens, what are my problems as a novelist? Similar to those of the Catholic? Quite different? Shall I find myself more restricted in my writing than the cheerful creature who rejects my belief, my passion; who thought his Mum and

Dad perfectly fine and sees all this couch-work as unnecessary, unhealthy, and morbid?

The answer is as before. If psychiatry were my love, I should write in the atmosphere of my love. Explicitly when it suited me; implicitly always. My danger would be no more than a variation of the chronic danger. I should, I mean, have to keep a watch on the technicalities, to present them clearly. If, for example, I wrote 'The exegesis of the affect' and expected anyone outside my field to understand me, I'd be very silly. I might, of course, be tempted to wave the Freudian flag too wildly. If I arranged in my early chapters, a maladjusted group; if I set down among them a kind, wise psychiatrist who fixed them all up and got thanked by everyone in the end, it wouldn't be a very good novel. It would be a sentimental novel. Just as it would be if, in my true allegiance, I set up a group of perfectly horrible Protestants and got them all converted in due course by a kind, wise old priest, so they lived cosily in the Catholic faith ever after. (If to be a Catholic is cosy, by the way, I am my Aunt Minnie.)

Politics, now. Were I passionately political, with a firm belief in this or that Party, what would be the chief snag lying between my party loyalty and my duty to my work as a novelist? I'm inclined to think the main hazard would be made by anger. The political animal is an angry animal. He's fighting a war all the time.

I have said I pray for anger. Do I pray for it to state itself in my work? Should an angry novelist write angrily? From the literary point of view, it is, I think, a mistake. And yet . . . and yet . . . I am not wholly wedded to the English distrust of hot blood. *'Had Mr. Snarl treated his subject with more coolness and detachment, he would have strengthened his case instead of weakening it.*' True or false?

Well, possibly both; the way some things—most disconcertingly—are.

Can one write well in anger; in hatred? I have one example in mind; an example with which I myself was concerned. I will tell the story, but I am bound by manners and prudence, not to mention the ties of friendship and the laws of libel, to give the characters certain disguises. They'll be called A., B. and C. To avoid confusion, I shall go on being I.

3

The time was the Thirties. The place was London. A. and B. were both friends of mine. A. was my friend first and came in time to disapprove mightily of my friendship with B. Since they seldom met, I didn't find it difficult to navigate between the two. I noticed that B. seemed to like A. and to remain unconscious of his disapproval. B., though he led a complex life, was at heart a simple person; he wouldn't necessarily expect to be liked, but it would surprise him to be hated. A. was a man of passionate, whirling loyalties.

Both were writers, both serious performers. A. wrote full-time. B. had a position in, let us say, a bank; he wrote with distinction and achievement in his spare hours.

The inevitable happened. A.'s dislike and distrust for B. presently began to take over, to work inside his head. Everywhere, it seemed to him, he found evidence that B. was the worst kind of monster and this invaded him with a growing compulsion to write about B. as he really was, to unmask the monster.

If you care to look back to Chapter One of this book, you'll find my observation that it's dangerous for me to draw a life-portrait because, once I've decided that a real person will be useful, I find it hard to refrain from giving my character *all* his qualities. His yellow socks, I point out, may creep in without my conscious intent. And in the next paragraph I suggest the concealment of a life-portrait by changing the chosen victim's looks and profession.

Did A. take any such precautions? Goodness me, no. B.'s looks, B.'s writing career, and B.'s daily job went straight in as they were. Nor was this all. He wasn't content to tilt only at B. and draw the rest of the cast from imagination. He put B.'s background, B.'s wife, and all B.'s girl-friends, myself among them, in too.

A.'s hatred had become a ruling passion. To write the story must have been a relief, a catharsis, besides—naturally—a lot of fun. It went to his head. He represented B. as dirty, unpopular, stingy, greedy, and wholly without talent: a liar, a sponger, a *noceur* somewhat handicapped by impotence, a painstaking deceiver of his good simple wife and all his girl-friends. In more dispassionate mood A. might have stopped to cock a detached eye. But he stopped not for stick and he stopped not for stone; he just threw them all at B.'s head as hard as he could.

When he had finished the story—and, I should imagine, long before—A. saw the danger of publishing it. I don't believe he feared that B. would sue him for libel. Certain problems in B.'s private and professional life were likely to dissuade him from a law-suit. But it was easy for the author to forecast the effect of this piece on a number of people, one of whom was me. What to do? Naturally he couldn't just keep the story dark in a drawer; who could?

What A. did first was to hand the typescript around among a few close friends; I was not (surprise, surprise) one of these. He swore them to secrecy. They showed a distinct loss of nerve. One managed to persuade him to change the banking job for another profession. Then they just sat and twittered. A. reassured them by saying he realised he couldn't publish the story in England. He would send it to America and sell it there.

As things turned out, he couldn't sell it there, which must have been baffling in the extreme. The English market was the only alternative. And in due course he got an offer from an English magazine. He accepted it. In A.'s position I would, I'm sure, have done the same; shutting my eyes tightly to the consequences ahead.

All this time, of course, I had lived, as B. had lived, in ignorance of the high-explosive threatening us both. I'd seen A. regularly and there was never a word of it until, having invited me to one of his elegant dinner parties, he asked me to stay behind after the others had gone, so he could make his confession.

Not a complete confession, you may be sure. Still he told me enough to make me uneasy. I was always afraid of A. I didn't ask for more details than he gave me, though I suspected him of soft-pedalling. He emphasized that this was meant to be a funny tale and that B. with his sense of humour would find it funny. Of course, A. reminded me, we all knew B. was a great liar and romancer; this aspect of him was the story's main theme. For example, the fellow in the story had a stock romance about the tragic death of one of his children, whereas in fact his whole family was alive and kicking.

A.'s merry laughter ran down while I stared at him in silence.

When you hate, you open the doors to influences far beyond your own control. Particularly when you let your hatred come down on paper. I can't remember if this was the first time I made the discovery. I know I've made it often since. Now, beside the fire in A.'s living-room, I sat plunged in horror. I heard myself mutter 'You put that in . . .'

A. looked startled.

'It happened to him—surely you knew it.'

'Oh God!'

'You didn't know?'

'I *swear* I didn't.'

I told him the story, adding miserably, 'It goes on being B.'s worst haunt, the death of those two babies.'

I watched A. bang his head with both hands. I watched him pace the room. He went on saying 'I swear I never knew.' I believed him; I still believe him.

'Couldn't you take it out? Just that one thing? Please . . .'

He stopped pacing. He looked haggard now, and haunted.

'I can't. I would, if I could. But the story comes out this week.' He told me the name of the magazine. It had a large circulation.

This week . . . I understood. He had told me only because I was bound to know.

I remember sitting on the floor in my Chelsea flat, reading the story. It was very long. I was hypnotized. I can remember no emotion at all; not even when I came to me (in my Chelsea flat); my character was a silly, masochistic young woman. She was called Agatha.

Even the illustrations presented a good likeness of B. Somebody had tipped the artist off. B. was in the habit of carrying a walking-stick; a particularly recognisable kind of cane; the artist had even reproduced the cane.

I remember that when I got up off the floor I was stiff from sitting so still.

Memories of the time immediately afterward are a little blurred. I remember that A. went into a nursing home, which would, come to think of it, have been more natural behaviour on the part of B. I went to see him there. I know I announced myself by the name of Agatha What-ever and that he blinked. I repeated it. He said 'Well, I *did* say you were beautiful.' He still frightened me; I couldn't make myself fight him as he deserved to be fought. He said one very odd thing: 'Won't you, yourself, take it to B. and show it to him?'

I said I would not. I added that this would be unneces-sary in any case; half a dozen of his best friends would have sent it to him by now. I was right. By evening the battle was on. The talk, in our close circle, was tremendous. I had the suspicion that a lot of people were enjoying them-selves immensely. I can remember the literary party, the eyes turning my way, the quick, eager questions. I put on an absurd, and I should think wholly unsuccessful act, shrugging and saying in an airy tone 'Oh—just think what fun it must have been for A. to write.'

The act didn't last beyond that particular evening. I saw B. the day after. He was deeply hurt; he sat like a stunned child, wondering why this had been done to him. Presently he said, 'Now listen . . . A. has never been a close friend of mine—which makes this attack all the more puzzling. But he is a very dear and old friend of yours. I don't want you to break with him on my account.'

My answer was short, and in one syllable.

Presently the buzzing died down. B. never brought the libel suit, though London's top lawyer advised him to do so. I severed relations with A. And hated him. It was a carefully nourished hate. It became a passion that raged at the going down of the sun and in the morning for nearly nine years. Not so B. He was a placid type and it didn't take him long to forget all about A.; more, I think, from his natural absent-mindedness than from any particularly Christian motive.

Now it was my turn to get my hatred on paper. Not enough for me to cut A. when I saw him, to blast him aloud when I heard his name. The obvious revenge was to hand; I made my plans for getting after him in print. One amusing way to do it, I thought, would be to knife him in the magazine where his own story had appeared. Meanwhile, I had a light novel in view. Conveniently I managed to include some outstanding 'A.' characteristics in a composite portrait which emerged as ludicrously as I intended. I rolled two other acquaintances up with A.—and it is a fact that both these originals called on him to offer condolence when the book appeared.

Now for the short story. Here I enjoyed myself, painting a sympathetic portrait of B. The theme was his absent-mindedness. A. was a novelist who libelled him and B. forgot all about it, making A. look a perfect ass. The story was sent to the relevant magazine. The editor, whom I knew, telephoned me, sounding a little careworn, to invite me to lunch.

When he asked me if I was deliberately gunning for A., my act was convincing enough. After all, a year had gone by. It wasn't difficult. I pretended not to know what he was talking about. He reminded me of A.'s story. I blinked several times; I frowned and finally appeared to remember. 'Oh . . . *that*. Goodness, I'd forgotten.'

'You had?'

'I promise. But now, of course, I see what you mean. Yes, yes, yes. How funny . . . never occurred to me.'

He seemed to believe this. Warming to my work, I began to tell him how my original idea had come to mind. I did it well. The editor declared himself quite satisfied with my string of lies. He hoped I hadn't thought him pusillanimous or fussy. He published the story.

Later that same year, the first magic of a novel moved in. I carried the dream of it to France and began to set it down on paper while I was there. Who was the stock villain of the piece? You'd never guess: it was A. Back in London, I wrote merrily and devotedly. It was a long book, and serious.

As I worked, I found myself succumbing to the familiar temptations. I didn't fight at all. In went A.'s physical characteristics; in went his marriage; and a good deal of his early background. Some of this, inevitably, came without my conscious knowledge or consent. Still, it came. About the only thing I didn't do to him was make him a writer.

Certain twinges, certain qualms, made themselves felt from time to time. I wasn't sure this portrait was kind or wise, though I would have gone bail for its being true. When I finished the book, I cast around in my mind. Where did we go from here? With a certain delight I chose two of the friends who had been privileged to read A.'s story in typescript . . . four years ago now. Solemnly I asked for their views. They began to scream. My telephone turned red-hot. They sent back the book. Hysterical little notes in the margins begged me to reconsider my more malicious touches.

Sulking, I consulted B. He didn't read it right through, as the others had. He didn't need to. He took a dart here and there, looking rather like a humming-bird who had connected with the sour instead of the sweet. After a while he put the script aside.

'How much revenge is there in this?' he asked me.

I told him.

He shook his head.

'Why shouldn't I?'

'It's on my behoof' (one of his words), 'is it not?'

'Well, naturally. I don't, as you know, incline to take revenge on my own—er—behoof.'

'It won't do.'

'Why won't it do?'

He stared past me. He murmured, *Vengeance is mine; I will repay, saith the Lord.*'

I wouldn't take that. He became explicit. He reminded me of some of the purely spiteful phrases I had used. 'When you come to making fun of a person's physical characteristics—' he paused.

'Well . . . A. did that to you.'

'So? Are you going to use *his* weapons?'

'Damn', I said. 'You win.'

I spent a few days cutting the worst. When the novel came out, A. heard about it from one of the two friends privileged to read the typescript. With commendable caution he decided not to read it.

War came. B. died in 1940. Several times before his death, he had asked me to make my peace with A. But I was still nursing my hatred and his death could only make the hatred stronger. It wasn't until 1944 that I met A. again. When A. asked my forgiveness, I looked over my shoulder and saw something strange. All this time I'd been vowed to hatred; I had brandished it for anyone who cared to see. I remembered somebody asking me during an air-raid, 'How are things between you and A. now?', and myself answering gaily, 'Well, I trust the biggest one the Germans have got aboard falls on him tonight.' And now it was over; it had been over for a long while; hatred had withered away. I had been holding on to the husk of it. No more. My voice sounded like B.'s when I said 'But of course, I've forgiven you—ages ago.' And it was true. And I've never hated, nor felt I had to forgive anybody, since. It was all learned in one lesson, and that was God, with a possible assist from B. but certainly none of my doing.

4

Which ought to be the end of the story. It isn't. I rather wish it were, except for the purposes of this chapter in this book.

More than ten years later, I met C. in New York. C. is a young relative of A., and I've known C. since she was a child; she is now an intermittent, though talented, writer. Over dinner she told me she'd just finished a book. She was also on her way to Europe. 'Shall you be seeing A.?' I asked unthinkingly.

'That depends.' She gave me a slanted look and giggled. 'On what?'

'On whether A. gets to hear about my novel.'

'What is this novel?'

She became rather cagey and mumbly. Presently she said, 'It's funny . . . Just so's A. can see it's meant to be funny,' and refused to go further.

Where, I asked myself, had I heard this sort before?

Well, of course: all those years ago: 'B. will find it funny.' I indulged a moment's reverie.

I ordered C.'s book before I left New York. Curiosity compelled me. So it reached me in London, first an unidentifiable parcel from America, then a hypnotizer that kept me sitting still on the floor of my flat in St John's Wood. I had plenty of work to do. But the paper on the desk seemed unimportant. I sat where I was. Once or twice I rose because I was getting stiff or because a phrase in the book pilloried A. so cruelly that I had to stand up and say aloud to C., 'Look here—you *can't* . . .' It had a hideous fascination. I think I ate dinner around nine-thirty p.m.

It wasn't that I found the novel a masterpiece. I had no immediate judgement—or was conscious of none. I was merely reading a satiric portrait of uncommon cruelty, as I'd read one sitting on another floor in Chelsea a long time ago. The wheel had come full circle. C.'s attack on A. began, I thought, where A.'s attack on B. had left off. I wished C. hadn't done it; and when I shut the book I was aware that my sympathies were with A. Still a demon behind my shoulder whispered, 'Justice . . . isn't it . . . after all?'

C. had sufficient sense not to publish the book in England. But within a remarkably short time copies came over the water. The battle was on. As when A. published his story and tongues wagged, I saw that a lot of people were enjoying themselves mightily. I wrote as much to A., who had taken the attack on the chin. But all was not well between A. and me because I wouldn't wholly condemn C. for writing it. Soon it became A.'s turn to cut me out of his life.

Why wouldn't I condemn C.? Because C. is a writer, and malicious portraits are the habit of writers when compulsion takes them. I'm not saying this is a good thing to happen; I merely know it does happen. Call it a demon, call it the devil's work, call it anything you like. I think of Maugham flaying Hugh Walpole. I think of H. G. Wells flaying Odette Keun. I think of A. flaying B. And I think of myself flaying A. There, but for the grace of God, we go . . . all of us.

(How would I have judged C.'s book supposing that A. had never flayed B.? Well, that's the sixty-four thousand dollar question.)

Some day, I imagine, I may find myself pilloried in a novel. The day hasn't come yet. I didn't set much store by the silly Agatha who was A.'s small portrait of me, because I was too busy crusading for B. But a full-length portrait, written in hate . . . how would that take me? I suppose my sense of proportion might collapse. But Lord, let me remember how. Lord, let me remember why. Lord, let me consider the occasion when I have had the same ungentlemanly fun. Lord, let me laugh.

Several years have passed since C.'s book came out. As far as I know, there has been no armistice yet between A. and C. A. is once more my friend, though I suspect I made a wound that will never entirely heal.

And now we are at the end of the saga; except for the literary summing up—and the postscript.

Was A.'s story the worse for the hatred that inspired it and rode it blind? Yes, it was. The portrait, as I have indicated, was loaded down with all the vices A. could muster. I remember hearing opinions from two people who had no clue to the situation, no idea that I was involved with it. One said, 'What on earth was all that burble about?' and the other said, 'I didn't get the point.'

Now to me: to my deliberate essays in malice. Did I

213

write the worse for being committed to hate? I did. In the light novel my slant matters less because the whole fabric is a patchwork of intentional nonsense, a near-farce. Even so, the 'A.' characteristics don't harmonise with the rest of the composite portrait; they stick out a mile. The serious novel remains forever weakened by my obsession. In a character who might have been solid and credible, there are false quantities, let in by hate; and nobody who read the book could, I think, believe that man ever existed.

And so to C. What's my assessment of her contribution to this chain of hate-literature? Remember, I'm still the guinea-pig for experiment: I can only give my own view.

What struck me most forcibly about C.'s book was that although it kept me hypnotized for an afternoon, I didn't believe a word of it.

What? How's that again? You just told us C. wrote a devilish attack on A.

I did; and this was so. But, you see, it didn't emerge as a true portrait from life. Possibly because C. had taken the precautionary measure of changing the character's looks and profession, I never saw the man as A. at all. And even though he wasn't the A. I knew, he didn't seem to be anybody else. Though his image obscured the true image, he never put on authentic flesh and blood of his own. During my afternoon's hypnosis, I could recognize many a theft from actual fact. I read remarks I'd heard before, picked up family jokes, saw real-life situations re-created. Scattered through the book were a few small incidents out of the past I'd shared with A. and C. But all this was like recognizing old snapshots in an album. I was engaged only in that highly superficial way. Not for a moment did I pass into the magic world of a novelist's making. Never was I caught up among the people in the story.

214

Never did I watch them, from the privileged position of the fly on the wall. My attention was, rather, distracted by the pattern on the wall-paper.

I fell between the book itself and the raw material from which the book was made.

This might be an illustration of the odd paradox: that to put fact into fiction most often produces an effect of unreality. But I don't think so. Though I've never heard how C.'s novel affected readers more innocent than myself, my guess would be that they found its story credible.

I've said that, as a writer, the scene clearest to my own eyes is the hardest to make lucid and visible on paper. With C.'s book, I think it was exactly the same state of affairs in reverse. As a reader, this time, the original was so clear to me that I couldn't get a picture from the printed page.

My postscript would remind you that A. behaved monstrously, with the result that I behaved monstrously and that, in due course, C. behaved monstrously. In fact, the only person who comes out of the proceedings well is B. Odd, when I reflect that the whole story began because A. decided B. was a monster.

CHAPTER

TEN

1

The world—or my own island? The circus of life, or the Ivory Tower? Where does my choice lie?

'*Just stay on the outside and watch it all. No need to get involved.*' I can still hear the echo of those words, still re-live the doubts they dropped into my mind. I was sixteen. It was my father who said this to me: a precept for the writer.

Instinctively I knew it for a precept I couldn't follow. I was still at school; the opportunities for becoming deeply involved were, you might think, somewhat limited. But so was my capacity for detachment. I knew it then as I know it now. Over the years I have not failed to discover how hard it is for me to be detached. Certainly there is the trained observer in my head, who watches drama like a lynx and will, when all's quiet again, be found to have recorded the scene. But I can never feel his presence so long as I am in the toils.

Despite the slow development, already noted, of moral indignation, I look back and see that I have been blazingly, painfully concerned with many matters outside myself and my writing. I don't mean merely being *busy* with them. I mean being enmeshed, drowned, wholly absorbed. The very reverse of 'staying on the outside and watching it all.' I have, I see, had many causes in my bones. And these are not the social or political causes into which moral indignation might properly have plunged me, but more random invaders of my peace. I have agonized for, and with, all sorts. Anything I am doing, work or play, I do with the whole of myself. I can see the younger versions of the present writer drowning; in the job at the Amalgamated Press when she was eighteen; in a crusade to rescue pedigree dogs (who, as it turned out, needed no rescue); in amateur theatricals; in photography; in the difficult art of public speaking; in a fight with England's biggest film-company to overset a verdict from the law-court; this I won. I have said my horizons were narrow. But within their limits my heart was hot. And there have been all kinds of agonies, worthless and worthwhile. The work beyond my own: a brief spell in Public Relations; the B.B.C.; the Ministry of Food in wartime. It has never been a matter of my sopping them up like a sponge. Each in its time has sopped up me.

The Army . . . My love-affair with the Army began as soon as I put on my hideous khaki clothes and became the oldest private in captivity. The Ministry of Food was at once forgotten. The training-centre was the world. The Officers' Training Unit where I went later to work for my commission, was another, wider world; but equally obsessive. I might have been eighteen years old and not thirty-four. Seldom can there have come within those grim Scottish walls a more devout cadet.

I am, except while cooking, singularly badly co-ordinated. If you're so made, it is obvious that you'll find drill

difficult and your marching will make your comrades gig-
gle. I was, among four hundred, the only cadet who found
it natural to swing my right arm and right leg concurrently.
This was the subject of a poem that contained the lines:

'Though my right arm, anatomy eschewing,
Will know—and do—what my right leg is doing.'

But I wrote the poem long afterwards. At the time I
couldn't laugh. I simply gave myself up as hopeless on the
parade-ground. So, I thought, did everybody else.

I couldn't, then, have been more surprised when I was
voted into a place of honour for our Passing Out Parade
(a ceremony which always seems to me oddly named).
I was to act as Company Commander. I should *lead* a
squad of khaki women, giving them their orders as we
filed past the saluting-base. Left Wheel, Eyes Right, Eyes
Front and all that . . . I felt as if I had won the Nobel
Prize. Excitedly, proudly, I joined the parade-rehearsal.

Nobody knew how serious I was about this rehearsal.
On the contrary. My company thought I was taking it all
as a great big joke. I can hardly blame them because in
my excitement I did everything that could be done wrong,
wrong. I set off on the right (which was the wrong) foot.
I forgot to wheel them at the corner. I gave them Eyes
Front for Eyes Right and in due course omitted to halt
them, so for a moment it looked as though they would
march straight into a high stone wall.

Even so I was quite unworried when the practice ended.
It was only a rehearsal and I knew from experience of my
own nervous-system that I should now 'be all right on the
night.' Had I done it perfectly, on the other hand, I should
have been full of jitters.

218

The Regimental Sergeant-Major, a neat cock-robin of a woman with an amiable smile, dismissed us. She beckoned me out of the line. She invited me to walk with her through some sacred-to-Officers precinct and I went along, grinning like a fool. Once we were away from the others, she broke the news. Gently she explained that I couldn't, after all, be trusted with so important a role in the parade. She couldn't risk mistakes. She asked me to step down in favour of Cadet H, not a friend of mine. It *would* be H, I said to myself as all the lights in my absurd sky went out. What could I do but submit? This was the Army (Mrs. Jones) and no R.S.M. was likely to believe my sincere protest that it would be all right on the night. I made no such protest. Saluting the cock-robin, I withdrew. I then went to my room and cried.

'What *are* you doing?' asked my roommate, astonished to find me up there alone.

'Crying,' I snapped.

When I told her why, she ceased to be sympathetic. She was stunned.

'How can somebody like you care about something like that?'

'Somebody like me *means* somebody who cares about something like that,' I assured her moodily. She was not convinced. She reminded me of my true career and the number of books I'd published. But these, I said, couldn't be less relevant. Then she used a phrase that reminded me of my father's old advice: something about standing aside, watching things happen; always a watcher, just a little remote; that was how she thought of a novelist; spying on the world with sharp, detached eyes.

Useless to explain that I couldn't feel like a novelist. My horizons were bounded by Cadet Frankau who had made a nonsense of the drill. They continued to be this way. Throughout life at the O.C.T.U., Cadet Frankau remained a compound of *Beau Geste* and *The Youngest Girl at St Chad's.*

Although, once I graduated, I never made an orthodox, nor even a faintly well-disciplined officer, the Army stayed in my bones until war ended. When the time came to get out of uniform, I felt very peculiar indeed.

I remember the last day of my official existence as Senior Commander Frankau, A.T.S. The London depot for demobilization would, it was rumored, issue me with a thumping ration of cigarettes, clothing-coupons by the hundred, chocolate by the ton, a personal letter from King George the Sixth and, far less credibly, two pairs of nylons.

I reached the place at lunchtime. I was down in a gloom of memories from the past and small misgivings for the future. Everybody, I discovered, was off-duty till two o'clock. So I couldn't be processed yet. I was directed to the Officers' Club across the yard.

Here beside the bar, to my surprise, stood a fruit-machine, or one-armed bandit. These had been made illegal. In England now they were as rare as nylons—or rarer. With a glad gambler's whoop, I fell on its neck. Kind of the Army to give me this treat by way of farewell . . . The machine was full to the brim, too; bulging with the hopeful sixpences of those who had come before me. I remembered the last time I had played one of these machines: at a country club in Sussex two years back, with a friend later killed in action. The club was raided; he and I had made a discreet escape in the dark. Blowing a kiss to his ghost, I put in my sixpence and pulled the lever.

There was a long, resounding clash-clash, tinkle-tinkle.

Sixpences showered down all over the floor. I had got the jackpot.

2

'The jackpot . . . You're making it up.'

  'I don't believe there was a fruit-machine at all.'

  'It's too bloody neat to be true.'

The fourth person present said, 'No, it's not. It's just one of those things that go on happening to Pamela. "She shall have drama wherever she goes,"' he added in a rather disagreeable tone.

True. It has been true for most of my life. And it isn't all jackpots. It is my fate to be vicariously accident-prone; or, if you prefer it, present-at-accident prone. Is anybody going to crash his car, fall off a ladder, slump to the ground in a fit? Then you can count on my being within a few yards of him. Dog-fights, children who get their fingers caught in things, fainting women, persecution-maniacs, expectant mothers going suddenly into labour:—these are not all. There are also the people who have just had their pockets picked, received bad news, lost their dogs, got in the wrong train, or left all their jewellery in a Ladies' Cloakroom.

When the adventures occur, I 'plug in' all too easily. I am wired to the person in distress and to the distress. Afterwards I remain haunted. The world, or this microcosm of it, is so much with me that I might have no other life. Once again I'm incapable of detachment.

Is this the way a novelist ought to be? If the emergencies themselves are part of a psychic pattern, should not the writer be grateful? Does it not give him the chance, time after time, to absorb the stuff of life—urgently, precipitately, for his own purposes? I only know that I always loathe it when it happens; and that it goes on happening. ('You *make* it happen, don't you see?' said my Freudian friend.)

I am also less mysteriously involved. Committee-work, meetings, agendas, reports, speeches on public platforms: all these have been among the results of my belated moral awakening. How often in the past few years has it been put to me that this takes time and energy away from my true task? Pretty often. I don't really need reminding. There's a two-way struggle inside my head.

Meanwhile I long for the Ivory Tower. This more and more with the years. My reveries always concern themselves now with a country house; somewhere in England or France, or on Martha's Vineyard.

Here I am living, lapped in quiet. I have a poodle, an Old English sheepdog, a cat and some rabbits. I am miles from a Highway or a town. I am protected by silent-footed, unobtrusive servants from the telephone, the laundry and the front door bell.

My study has soundproof walls. In England, the radio and the television will stay switched off until the cricket season begins; and return to their silence as soon as the season ends, four and a half months later. In France, as in America, there would be neither radio nor T.V.

Newspapers will not be read. The London *Times* crossword puzzle will be cut out and placed on my breakfast tray every morning. Once a week my secretary will hand me an intelligent report of the world news, a note of the deaths, a summary of the new books and plays. The secretary will, of course, keep entirely out of my life besides having none of her own. Like the servants, she must be silent, unemotional, odourless and orderly. She must never know a day's illness; and this goes for the animals too.

I shall walk in my garden. I shall drive my car, very slowly, to the village, to Mass, to the top of a hill in spring-time. Aside from breakfast I shall cook my own food as and when I feel like eating. The servants will do the dishes.

Reading the *Times* (the house-agents' advertisements being right beside the crossword) I find myself regularly rivetted.

> SHROPSHIRE. In unspoilt country, two miles from pretty village. Small Georgian house fully modernized, in perfect condition. Two bedrooms; two bathrooms; two gracefully proportioned reception rooms with original panelling. Large studio-room at back (suit artist or writer). Fully equipped, modern kitchen. Oil-fired central heating. Servants' cottage in grounds (about thirty acres, with matured garden; small orchard and trout-stream).

We're off. I'll sell the Hampstead house tomorrow. Slowly, scrupulously, I make my plans. The details fall into place. And it takes some truly formidable snag (what, for example, does one do about a hairdresser?) to wake me up. I needn't, I realize, worry about the hairdresser. This is just a pipe-dream—a game I play. Not a life, but an imagined escape from life.

Should I really pull up stakes and go to live in country solitude, I wouldn't find the thing I want. The house would become as demanding as any other home. The household, human and animal, would step up anxiety or irritation—or both. Life would move in; reality would bring people and crises and 'ills and cross-accidents.' If I didn't know this (and I do) I need not look far to see a proof of it.

Because I shared this particular reverie with another writer. He was a neighbour of mine in Hampstead and together we would indulge our similar pipe-dreams. Four years ago he went after his. He found the house; he bought it, 'and I shall live,' he said, 'like a monk in a cell.'

It is by all accounts a beautiful cell. Those who visit him return in envious raptures. They describe his study; they describe his garden; they talk of the lake and the trees and the silence. They tell me he has the perfect house-keeper and the kind of effortlessly wonderful secretary you read about in novels. But the last time I heard of him he was building himself a cottage at the end of the garden to get away from the house.

And I do see . . . There's no escape, no Ivory Tower, except the one inside.

3

This is the place to preserve at all costs, the silent place of your own in your head. You may be blown every which way by the winds of the world. You may be doomed to drama, like me; susceptible to other people's small agonies, like me; incapable of detachment, torn to pieces. Yet you can still preserve your inner silence, your own private tower.

How? How can a writer do that?

The actual protection of the dream, the idea unfolding, is such a personal affair that I can give only tentative suggestions. Not too many people; not too many drinks; not too much talk; ration your reading of contemporary novels. That's about all. The dream, once it decides to stay, has a

224

habit of protecting itself. And for the Rough, my chosen beginning, I have outlined the forms protection must take. Equally, for the Smooth. Your methods may differ greatly from mine. But, no matter what methods we use, there is one lesson to be learned by all of us; the basic lesson. Having learned it, we can hold our citadel.

I mean absolute, complete concentration.

When I began writing, I had no room of my own to which I could retreat. There was a nice large living-room for the family; and there was a gramophone. I wrote, curled up in a corner of the sofa, and it would have been unthinkable to ask for the gramophone to be turned off.

Aside from this, there was only the commuter's train between Windsor and London. In the third-class carriage on the 8:36 there was little elbow room; even less on the 6:38 coming home. But these were the working-sites for two novels and I cannot think of a better discipline. I can still write pretty well anywhere. If you teach yourself to do this I think you will find, as I have found, that the lion-strength of your impulse carries you on. The magic pull of your second life is probably the *only* thing that can draw you right away from the surrounding racket.

As soon as I sold my first novel, I bought a first-class season ticket for the commuter's train. The resulting elbow room was bliss. But there was a new hazard. In the crowded third-class carriage none of the jam-packed passengers had ever asked me what I was doing. (Sometimes I became aware that one was reading over my shoulder and when this happened I would write a rude word in legible letters.) But in the luxury class I would often find myself alone with just one other person. That person would almost invariably ask me what I was writing. When I said a novel he would begin to interview me about the difficulties of doing this on a train:

'I mean—don't you find it awfully hard to concentrate?'

It was on the Windsor-London journey, on a Sunday evening, that my powers of concentration nearly killed a large Portuguese gentleman. The train was blessedly empty. The first-class carriages stayed unvisited by all but me. I took my pick of them. I settled down to work in a corner seat. As the train moved I saw, out of the tail of my eye, a shadow cross the far window. I went on writing. The train moved faster. I became aware of a distinct draught blowing. It went on blowing. After a moment, I glanced peevishly in the direction of the draught and saw that the far door was hanging open, with a man clinging to the handle, falling out backwards.

I don't remember pulling him in. There was a complete black-out in my head. The next thing I knew was the two of us glaring at each other like a couple of bears, on hands and knees on the floor of the carriage, with the open door slam-banging away behind the large gentleman's shoulder. Another ten seconds and I would have been too late. ('Just one of those things that go on happening to Pamela.')

It is more imperative to teach yourself the lesson of absolute concentration now than it ever was before, because there's more noise than there ever was before. The kindest gift one could make to a struggling writer today would be to keep him in ear-plugs. Noise has, however, been a doom of mine since I began. I look back across years of sitting down in rooms all over the map; sitting down in comparative quiet, pen in hand. After a very few minutes somebody begins to play the piano, take out the boiler from the kitchen downstairs, lay a carpet, start up a motor-bicycle that won't start, use a buzz-saw, demolish a small shed. When I first settled in California the neighbours took one look at me sitting down to my desk and then tore their own house up by the roots. In London I once got a flautist in the flat next to mine, a piano on the floor above, and the playground of a boys' school below the windows. I pressed on: there was nothing else to do; I had taken the flat for six months. Presently, on the large empty plot just beyond the school, they began to build a synagogue.

I have to admit that I owe to the noise-doom my capacity for concentrating in spite of it. It persists, but by and large I have won. When I worked at the Ministry of Food, early on in the war, the Ministry was hit by a bomb. Next day the workmen did their rapid emergency repairs and all in my department were given the afternoon off because nobody, it was agreed, could work through the barrage of sound. I had a rush job to do. I was writing my only authentic, though unsigned, best-seller. It was the Ministerial publication *Food Facts From the Kitchen Front,* a collection of wartime recipes and hints for the British housewife. My task was to turn the unwieldy and assorted idiom into English. (Rather fun, really. There comes to mind one phrase most urgently in need of translation: 'To be self-supporting, you need to grow quite a patch of parsley.')

Reluctantly I had to decline my chief's permission to quit the cook-book for the afternoon. Certainly the noise was terrible; but I couldn't in honesty plead that it would hold me up.

My father was of the generation who wrote in an ordained silence, not even the vacuum-cleaner allowed to perambulate outside the study door. His ruling forbade any interruption whatsoever from nine-thirty till one-fifteen. He said to me once, 'If I heard that you and your

227

sister had been killed in a street-accident, I wouldn't leave my desk a minute before that.'

I said, 'I don't see how you could possibly hear the news a minute before that.'

It was he who taught me to be industrious. But he could never teach me, in youth, to keep his own regular working hours. I have never learned to keep them. Nor can I make them a precept for you who are starting out today. The working programme is another personal affair. You may be like me—erratic, over-excited; liable when opportunity comes to write ten hours at a stretch; equally likely to write only four hours next day. You may, as I had to, work at another job and write your novel in your spare time.

After I came to live in London, just over thirty years ago, the commuter's train looked, in retrospect, like a refuge. I had to make a different daily pattern. I can remember leaving the advertising agency at five-thirty every evening and embarking on the interval for playtime. Whether it was a theatre, a movie, a dinner-date, ice-skating or dancing, it could only be an interval. After it I went to my desk; writing till two or three a.m. with a pot of black coffee at my elbow. My office day began at nine. This is the kind of thing you can do while you are young. But to be truthful I must record that the routine worked for just two years. At the end of which time I was not only as thin as a rail and perpetually hollow-eyed, but had got the sack from the advertising agency.

Whatever the day, wherever you are, you should, I think, aim to write for a minimum period of two hours.

Those two hours must belong to you absolutely. You won't find it easy to persuade anybody else how sacred they are. It was Dorothy Parker who said to me, 'Tell your friends you can't see them because you've a date for a manicure, and they say, "Why, sure, darling—some other time." Tell them you're working and they say, "I'll be right over."'

You must, as my father tried to teach me long ago, be selfish. Not only selfish: bloody, bold and resolute. And this must go on all your life, because, take it from me, the insidious pleadings never let up. 'I won't keep you more than ten minutes,' is one of them. Perhaps the most tiresome, when I have made it clear that I daren't come out to lunch, can't come out to lunch, won't come out to lunch, is 'Well, you've got to eat *somewhere*, haven't you?' The answer's No. But if, like me, you resent having to be rude, you'll find it hard to say.

Speaking for my middle-aged self, the most perplexing hazard is made neither by noise nor by the attempted invasions. I cannot remember its being a hazard in youth. It is the intermittent necessity to write in hotel rooms and other people's houses. Both are equally unlikely to provide a writing table. I cannot imagine how anyone dependent on a typewriter finds anywhere to put it. I have at least my faithful writing-board, foolscap size with a clip at the top to hold the pages. (Bought from M. C. Flynn, New York, ten years ago, and now so much a part of me that to lose it would amount to a physical amputation.) Even so, ingenuity is required; especially if I'm engaged on the Smooth which, as indicated, needs a long, solid surface. I do try to keep the Smooth at home, but sooner or later will come a time when it has to take its chance abroad.

The trick here is to get three chairs lined up. I lay the notebook on one chair, the Rough on the other and sit in the third, balancing the board on my knees. This is a comparatively simple matter in an hotel, where one can always ask for an extra chair.

In an alien house, the whole issue becomes astonishingly difficult. I can only think of two where it wasn't; in one of them I was empowered to annex the dining-room table because the cook had just given notice. As a rule, I am at once inhibited by the presence of a pretty little desk—or *escritoire* (a mysteriously onomatopoeic word). When I sit in front of it, the flap comes about a foot above my knee-level. The elbow room here is rather less than in that long-ago third-class carriage. A precious china ornament is liable to be standing on top of the little desk and this rocks slightly.

There are not, in the room, three chairs of corresponding height. Why should there be? There's a stool, perhaps, in front of the dressing table; like the one covered with priceless petit-point, on which I upset a bottle of ink in New Hampshire. I cannot imagine where I found the ink. I must have brought my own. That other people don't have ink is a fact I've established beyond dispute. (And if somebody wants to know what's wrong with using a ball-point pen, I'm prepared to explain, but not here, for the sake of the manufacturers' sensibilities.)

Next comes the lighting question. In an hotel it's easy to see why there's no light anywhere near the table because there isn't a table. But it's *not* easy to see why all lights in all hotel-bedrooms are muted to a regulation dimness—particularly the one for reading in bed. In the alien home, stronger bulbs are used. The problem is to get near one of them without moving too much of the furniture.

I met an unexpected challenge once on my own ground, Martha's Vineyard. Winter had caught up with us two days before the oil heating was to be installed. I had a scene to finish and I was going to finish it if I froze. Dressed in three sweaters, long woollen underpants, heavy trousers and fur boots, wearing a coat, a scarf, a Balaclava helmet, and a fur-lined glove on my left hand, I was hard at it when the builder arrived. He had come to check on some aspect of the heating installation. He asked me if I wasn't freezing to death. I said yes. Then why didn't I stop? Because I had to go on. He couldn't understand how anyone could be so crazy. I was moving to the hotel tonight, wasn't I? Yes. Then why not go now? Because I wanted to get the scene finished first. The conversation became a deadlock. I remember his saying, 'You're just obstinate, I guess.'

The same sort of obstinacy, I hope, as my father possessed. He had a book still to finish while he was dying; he shortened his life by weeks, working on it. But he got it done.

And now that this book is nearly done, I'll pause to look over my shoulder.

I observe rather more than the usual variety of backgrounds and background noises. True, it was begun in quiet, at Hove, Sussex, in my father's study—the perfect place for work, as I have said. But that silence soon gave way to the sound of drills and hammers at my ear, the crash of falling plaster on the staircase. The Hampstead house was being operated on for dry rot. (If you too have watched three men happily making a bonfire of what was your bathroom floor in the front of your garage-yard, you will understand my situation.)

When, defeated, I moved to an hotel in Baker Street, and installed a writing-table, some echo from Hampstead followed me. Only two men this time, but they were taking out the whole bathroom just across the corridor. After that I went to Birmingham (England not Alabama). The Railway hotel confounded me by having a writing-table of excellent size. There was however a rich train-life proceeding night and day under my window, which faced on to the tracks. Using my ear-plugs I could still hear the steam-whistles, the rattling and clanging and clunking: above it all, over the public-address system, was borne a faint, far, continuous voice urging passengers on to Sutton Coldfield.

Next month, Venice, Greece and the Dalmatian coast took my eyes and my mind off the manuscript for a little while. But in Dublin, beguiling though I find that city, the discipline returned. Then London again. And the last lap has brought me back to the United States, for the first time in almost three years. I have moved via New York, New Orleans, Carmel and San Francisco, back to New York again.

(For the record, the writing-table at Carmel was long and steady; silence endured. The lobby of the Hay Adams House, Washington, could accommodate the Smooth, because there was a wide sofa for the Rough and people talked quietly. Under my current windows, an all-day army of bulldozers, cranes and drills, with rhythmic blasts of explosive, helps to drown out the T.V. in the neighbouring room.)

With the end in sight, I can be happy. I recall once again that my lifelong dread is the dread of the work left unfinished. Does that sound like a form of pride? (After all, there was only one person, ever, who could say with truth, *'Consummatum Est'*.)

4

No, it isn't pride. There's a particular mental attitude here. I touched upon this at the end of Chapter Six when I wrote, 'Your concern is with a gift and the service of it.'

The preservation of the inner Ivory Tower, to which I devote my strenuous labours at a discipline, is not accomplished by taking myself seriously. Only by taking my work seriously.

If you are preoccupied with yourself as a person of importance, you will find obstacles coming between you and the quiet refuge in your head. In youth, egoism is rampant: a natural disability. It's imperative that you should see it as a disability—something you will lose in time, like your spots or your puppy-fat. There must come the moment when, as Brother Leo wrote, all your mirrors turn into windows. That is the moment of growing up. The adult can look outward; the adolescent looks inward.

The moment can be long delayed. An early success (like a loving family) can persuade you that you're somebody special. So persuaded, you will have much to learn and more, alas, to unlearn. Your own image will get in your way. The wide-angle lens through which you as a writer must look at the world won't do its proper work.

The cash coming in, the publicity-noises, the bandwagon, these are material rewards. All too easy in this day and age—and particularly in this country—to mistake them for achievement. The prevalence of prizes doesn't help. The current spate of Oscars and Tonys only reminds me of the Caucus Race in *Alice:* 'Everybody has won, and all must have prizes.'

But you don't need an Oscar to give you the fatal notion that you are now a personality. That can happen quite quickly, once success begins. When I use the word, by the way, I am not using it in its old, true sense. I am using it in the contemporary sense whereby it means a public figure, somebody recognisable, a star. America is adept at building up these false personalities and England is fast learning the trick.

Take it from me, please, that you the personality can only obstruct you the writer. Keep a strict watch on the temptation to cut public capers. You may start with the honest belief that these help to 'promote' your work. So they may. Yet you are likely to end by 'promoting' yourself, not only in the public eye but in your own. And that won't do.

Remember, above all, that the artist can and should be of public service without ever becoming public property.

Is there an exercise in the separation of yourself from your talent? Yes. It isn't an exercise you're likely to find in one of those three-hundred-dollar writing courses. But I offer it here.

No matter what you create, the creative gift itself remains a miracle. The word 'gift' is important: something that has been given to you, not something you yourself have achieved. To my way of thinking, it is a gift from God. To your way of thinking, it may be just a piece of luck landed from nowhere. Either way, it must be seen soberly and in true perspective.

In a sense, the gift belongs to you utterly; to nobody else. In another sense it doesn't belong to you at all; it has been entrusted to you. You are its steward.

Which may seem a pompous approach to the gift of writing fiction. Do I mean you should enshrine your talent as something to be worshipped night and day? Kneel down and say your prayers to your ability to write a serial for *Ladies Home Journal?* No, I don't mean that. I mean, keep careful watch. Be a good steward. It is most necessary now.

You and I are living in a time that increases the threat to the tools of our trade: the words. I feel rather less jolly today than I did when I talked in Chapter Seven of the American attitude to words. Stop, look and listen; and you will, I think, become aware of a hideous abasement in the language. And of worse: an actual decline in the demand for what you and I are seeking always to find: the right word on paper.

The age at which children learn to read is one ominous signal. Every normal child should be able to read before he's five years old. The methods by which reading is taught today are the obstacles to this natural development.

Move over into the adult world; you'll find the signs of illiteracy everywhere. And no wonder. When a poet wrote *The word, and naught else, in time endures,* he wasn't thinking of the commercials.

That non-stop movie screen in the home has a lot to answer for. It is the reason why you and I are witnessing the slow death of the living theatre. It is one source of a daily discount in the value of the imagination. Others before me, middle-aged for the most part, have deplored the signs of their times. But I doubt that there ever existed so evil an opportunity for misusing the creative gift as the appallingly-limited medium of television. These limitations may be temporary. But we condone them in all cosiness. T.V. is a thing-in-itself. (I shall carry with me for a while the sorrowful look of the bellhop who put down my luggage on the floor, then moved to the set to turn it on. When I told him I didn't use it, I had to repeat myself. After I'd said that a third time, he shook his head sadly and went away.)

I can only think of one bigger menace to sane society; and that's the H-bomb.

(I am aware that this isn't a popular view. The bomb, like T.V., is here. Mankind needs to make what is here a fact for rejoicing. Progress has brought us these things. Everything about us indicates progress, so everything must be fine. All that is newer, bigger, faster, must be right. The trees are cut down to make the Highway broader, so who would sorrow for the trees?)

Televised drama is not, by the way, a new phobia. I first met it as an enemy in Hollywood, 1940, and have seen no reason to change my opinion since. I am told that a hashed-up, mutilated version of a Shakespeare play can now reach millions of people. That's a good thing: that's progress. (Which, of course, it may be, in the current belief that a lot of something second or third rate is an improvement upon less of something first-rate.) What it *isn't*, let us remind ourselves, is Shakespeare.

Still, mustn't grumble. At least nobody has yet attempted to defend to me America's determined, nation-wide effort to combat one of the natural human needs: the need for silence. It's obvious that eyes dulled by watching television are not at their most receptive for the printed word. But how about ears dulled by the imposition of piped music? What can they hear—as the doom pursues them, in restaurants, in waiting-rooms, in shops, in airports, in the aircraft itself? Very little. I take back what I said earlier about the British being the worst listeners in the world. The Americans are now. They have to be.

Those who cannot hear themselves speak will soon not be able to hear themselves think. To think, we need a ration of silence. Silence in this country is at a premium. Who feels like paying the premium?

In the absence of an answer to my query, I'll content myself with this quotation from a brochure advertising an expensive motel:

236

There are three radio-positions in the dial on your desk, as well as Muzak. Muzak may also be heard under water in the pools, another first in the South-East.

On which merry note, it is time to end; reflecting that though you, today's writer, may be beset by more hazards and frustrations than ever I was, you can still be trusted to overcome them. If, that is, you say Yes always to your dream; and No always to the compromise the noisy world offers you in exchange.

For the time left to me, this must remain my own endeavour. If I betray it, then let my right hand lose its cunning.

C51